Threshold to Music

SECOND EDITION

Higher Grades Teacher's Resource Book

ELEANOR KIDD
MUSIC CONSULTANT
Richmond, California

Fearon•Pitman Publishers, Inc.
Belmont, California

Acknowledgments

Credit and grateful appreciation are due the publishers and owners for use of the following songs. Any omissions are due to the difficulty in finding the source of the material and can be corrected by contacting Fearon•Pitman Publishers, Inc., Belmont, California.

"Old Woman" from *Exploring Music, Books Two and Three,* by Eunice Boardman and Beth Landis, Holt, Rinehart and Winston, Inc., 1966.

"Camptown Races," Stephen Foster, from *Discovering Music Together, Books Three and Four,* by Beatrice Perham Krone, Charles Leonard, Irving Wolfe, and Margaret Fullerton. Copyright © 1966, 1973 by Follett Educational Corporation, division of Follett Corporation. Used by permission.

"We're Going 'Round the Mountain" and "Goodbye, Old Paint" from *Making Music Your Own, Books Two and Four,* Silver Burdett Company, Division General Learning Corporation, 1971.

"Brooms" from *The Ditty Bag* compiled by Janet Tobitt, used by permission.

Appreciation and thanks are also given to the teachers and pupils of the Richmond Unified School District, Richmond, California, for their cooperation and whole-hearted enthusiasm in providing many of the concepts presented in this book. My thanks also to John Hammett for invaluable assistance given with patience and good humor.

Cover Art: "Dog Barking at the Moon" by Joan Miró (Oil on Canvas, 1926). Reproduced by permission of the Philadelphia Museum of Art; the A. E. Gallatin Collection; Photo by Alfred J. Wyatt.

Edited by John Hammett
Illustrated by Hildy Burns and Darcy Paige
Photographs by John Monroe
Typography by Polycarp Press, San Francisco

ISBN-0-8224-9068-4

Printed in the United States of America

Foreword

Recent years have generated new insights concerning purposes and methods of music education. One of the major thrusts has been toward the totality of music education with special attention to music as it is heard, felt, imagined, and created. The aural nature of music is being placed once again in the center of the music experience. The development of aural acuity becomes the basis for improved performance, improvisation, and creative activities.

The *Threshold to Music, Second Edition,* exemplifies this contemporary emphasis in teaching music to children. Rhythmic comprehension, melodic contour, feeling for phrasing, and dynamics and pitch contrast are all approached through the ear and body movement.

Visual matters are presented only after aural recognition and body response have provided a foundation for musical learning. Inner hearing, seeing what one hears, and hearing what one sees are integral features of the lessons presented.

The program proceeds in sequential fashion, and lessons are carefully outlined in a way that makes them very attractive to classroom teachers who need such support to build confidence in teaching their own music. One of the outstanding features is the use of charts instead of books, making it possible for the teacher to pinpoint class attention on the concepts presented. Without concentrated eye involvement with the score as music is heard, studied, and sung, music reading ability will not develop. Thus, the use of such charts helps to overcome one of the weaknesses of much music teaching, and raises the level of music literacy.

Karl D. Ernst
Past President International Society for Music Education
Past President Music Educators National Conference
Past Professor Music Education, California State University, Hayward

Contents

Musical Terms

Accelerando Becoming faster.

Accent The stress of one tone over others, usually on the first beat.

Anacrusis Up beat or pickup which indicates a melody begins with an incomplete measure.

Andante A slow, even tempo; Italian for "going."

Bar Lines Lines dividing a certain number of beats into measures.

Beat The basic unit of time in music, usually organized in groups of two or three.

Cadence A musical resting place at the end of a phrase or section of a composition.

Canon A composition in which all parts have the same melody but start at different points.

Chord A simultaneous sounding of three or more tones.

Clef A sign written at the beginning of the staff to indicate the pitch of the note (𝄞 or 𝄢).

Crescendo A gradual increase in volume of sound indicated by the sign ◁ .

Da Capo Repeat the music from the beginning to the end. Abbreviated to D.C. and meaning "from the beginning."

Decrescendo A gradual decrease in volume of sound indicated by the sign ▷ .

Diatonic The order of notes as found on the white keys of the piano, using whole steps and half steps.

Dissonance A sometimes disagreeable effect produced by certain intervals or chords.

Dotted Notes A dot placed after a note receives half the value of the note it follows.

Double Bar Two vertical lines drawn through the staff to indicate the end of the section or composition.

Down Beat The downward motion given by the conductor to indicate the beginning beat of a measure.

Duet A composition for two performers of equal importance.

Dynamics Varying or contrasting degrees of intensity or loudness.

Eighth Note A unit of musical notation that receives one half the time value of the quarter note (♩).

Ensemble Cooperation of several performers.

Fine End or close.

Flat The symbol (♭) which indicates the lowering of the pitch by one half step.

Form The organization of all elements of a composition to achieve aesthetic logic.

Forte Italian word meaning loud and strong, abbreviated to *f*.

Fortissimo Very loud, abbreviated to *ff*.

Half Note The half note receives half the value of a whole note and receives two pulses when the lower number of the time signature is four.

Half Rest The sign (▬) indicating silence corresponding to the half note.

Inner Hearing Hearing the melodic or rhythmic pattern within the body without singing or playing.

Interval The difference in pitch between two tones.

Key Signature The sharps (♯) or flats (♭) appearing at the beginning of each staff which indicate the key of the composition.

7

Ledger Lines Short lines drawn through the stems of notes which are too high or low to be represented on the staff.

Measure The space between two bar lines.

Melodic Contour A melody pictured by a line drawing or other notation.

Meter The basic scheme of note values and accents which remain unaltered throughout the composition.

Mezzo Italian for middle or half, hence mezzo forte (*mf*) means half as loud.

Minuet A dance in 3/4 time that became the official dance of the French court in 1650. It soon became popular in America during the Revolutionary War.

Mystery Song Recognition of a familiar song by rhythm pattern.

Octave An interval consisting of eight diatonic notes.

Ostinato Italian, meaning stubborn. A clearly defined musical figure which is persistently repeated, usually by the same voice or pitch.

Pattern A succession of notes which forms a recognizable unit.

Pentatonic A scale of five tones with no half steps between any two tones. Related to the five black keys of the piano.

Phrase A natural division of the melodic line, comparable to a sentence in speech.

Piano Italian for soft, indicated by *p*.

Pianissimo Very soft, indicated by *pp*.

Pitch The location of a musical sound in a tonal scale, proceeding from low to high.

Quarter Note A unit of notation that receives one pulse when the lower number of the time signature is four (♩).

Quarter Rest A sign (𝄽) indicating silence corresponding to the value of the quarter note.

Repeat Sign A sign signifying that the music between 𝄆 and 𝄇 is to be repeated.

Rhythm Notes of different duration combined in sequence to create a pattern.

Rondo A composition characterized by the principal theme being repeated after each new theme is introduced.

Round A common name for a circle canon.

Scale The term, which means "ladder," denotes a succession of notes arranged in rising pitches.

Sharp The symbol (♯) which indicates the raising of a note by one half step.

Sixteenth Note A unit of musical notation that receives one half the time value of an eighth note (♪).

Solmization A method of teaching scales and intervals using syllables.

Staff A series of five horizontal lines on which musical notes are written.

Syncopation The deliberate upsetting of the normal pulse of meter, accent, and rhythm.

Tempo Italian for time, with regard to speed. Pace at which a composition is to be performed.

Tie A curved line placed over a note and its repetition to show that the two should be performed as one unbroken note.

Time Signature The time (meter) is indicated at the beginning of a composition in the form of a fraction. The denominator indicates the unit of measurement (half note, quarter note, etc.), while the numerator indicates the number of such units in a measure.

Tonality The sense of feeling the relationship of intervals to the beginning pitch.

Triad A chord of three tones.

Triplet A group of three notes performed in place of two notes of the same value and indicated by a three and a bracket ($\overset{3}{\sqcap}$).

Unison Playing or singing the same notes or melody at the same pitch or an octave apart.

Whole Note The largest single unit of modern musical notation receiving a value of four pulsations in meter (𝅝).

Whole Rest A pause or silence equal in length to a whole note (𝄻).

Introduction

The second edition of the *Threshold to Music* is greatly influenced by the pedagogy of Zoltán Kodály. In keeping with Professor Kodály's belief that all children should be provided with musical skills, this program will enable the teacher to present a developmental approach to the reading and writing of music.

To teachers:

who feel that the teaching of music is not one of their strengths, either through lack of experience or training, and therefore, lack of interest,

Who have little or no help from a music specialist due to scheduling or financial needs of the school district,

who feel there can be musical experiences other than the conventional "songbook-record" approach,

the *Threshold to Music* will provide a stepping stone to rewarding musical experiences involving singing, music reading, and participation.

The teacher of the self-contained classroom can have the greatest influence on a child's attitude to all learning. The teacher's enthusiasm, sense of humor, intelligence, and training can give the child experiences that cannot be duplicated. It is natural to teach from personal strengths, whether reading, language arts, science, art, physical education, or music. This is the natural desire in all of us—to be successful. Many times this desire leads to imbalance within the educational framework. Therefore, it would be ideal to have a "specialist" come into the classroom and "take over" those subject areas that are not one of the teacher's "strengths," but until that ideal becomes a reality, the classroom teacher must try to be all-knowing in the various programs offered in the schools.

For ease of planning, the *Teacher's Resource Book* contains a miniature of each classroom chart with each lesson. Although it might be a temptation to present the classroom charts at the beginning of each lesson, greater success will be achieves by the utilization of preparatory experiences. Rhythmic and melodic activities should be presented at the beginning of the school year, using familiar songs from previous experiences.

BASIC RHYTHMIC AND MELODIC ACTIVITIES

- Sing many songs—folk songs, camp songs, and spirituals.
- Start the day with a song, take a break with a song, create new words to a familiar song.
- Call the daily roll using *sol–mi* (*G* to *E* on the piano); the children will echo their name. For example,

Teacher sings	Mary echoes
Ma — ry	I'm here
(sol) (mi)	(sol) (mi)

- Use rhythmic activities at various times of the day, to relieve tensions, to provide a transition from one subject to another, to teach children to listen and follow directions, and to give children an opportunity for leadership. For example,

Sing a song and *clap* the **beat.**

Sing a song and *step* the **beat.**

Sing a song, *walk* the **beat,** *change direction* at the end of the **phrase.**

Sing a song and *clap* the **pattern** (syllables of the words).

- Build a musical vocabulary through a song to provide the children with experiences that will lead to success when presented with the classroom charts. See the list of "Musical Terms" presented in this book on page 7.

The *Preparation for the Chart* in the *Teacher's Resource Book* may be presented several days prior to introducing the charts to the class.

It will be obvious to those who read the material that each lesson presents more activities than can be accomplished successfully in a single music lesson.   *Other Songs to Use* and *Additional Activities* provide the teacher with a variety of enrichment experiences that will fit the needs and individuality of the students.

The second edition of the *Threshold to Music* will enable the classroom teacher to discover the excitement of learning how to learn through music. The involvement of the teacher and child in rhythm and song through the use of the classroom charts will provide musical perception and awareness that can be related to all learning. To understand the potential this program can offer, one need only remember the old Chinese proverb: "He who hears, forgets; he who sees, remembers; but he who does, knows."

E.K.

Music Moves Through Time

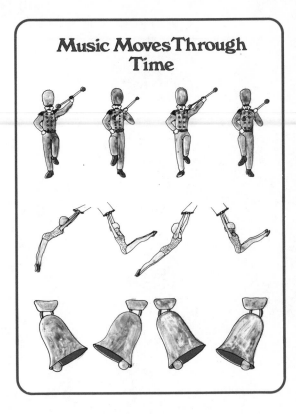

WHEN JOHNNY COMES MARCHING HOME

Patrick Gilmore

When John—ny comes march—ing home a—gain, Hur – rah! Hur – rah! We'll

give him a hear—ty wel – come then, Hur – rah! Hur – rah! The

men will cheer and the boys will shout, The lad – ies, they will

all turn out, and we'll all feel gay when John—ny comes march—ing home.

PREPARATION FOR THE CHART

When Johnny Comes Marching Home

1. Teach the song.
2. Sing the song and clap the **beat** (two beats to a **measure**).

   Note: The first beat occurs on the word "John." The word "When" is an **anacrusis** *or pick-up (see list of Musical Terms).*

   When | John—ny comes march—ing | home a—gain. *and so on.*

3. Sing the song and step the beat.
4. Sing the song and walk the beat; at the end of each **phrase** (⌒), change direction (this is called turning the phrase).

12

THE MAN ON THE FLYING TRAPEZE

American Tavern Song

sol

He flies through the air with the great — est of ease, The
dar — ing young man on the fly — ing trap — eze, His ac — tions are
grace — ful, all girls he does please, And my love he has sto — len a — way.

THE LITTLE BELLS OF WESTMINSTER

Traditional Round

sol

The lit—tle bells of West—min—ster go ding, dong, ding, dong, dong.

5. Sing the song, march the beat, keep the beat with an imaginary baton while turning the phrases.

The Man on the Flying Trapeze

1. Teach the song.
2. Sing the song and clap the first beat of each measure. This song also has an anacrusis):

He | flies through the | air with the |

     great—est of | ease, *and so on.*

Note: This is called clapping the **accent.**

3. Sing the song and keep the beat by swinging on an imaginary trapeze.

The Little Bells of Westminster

1. Teach the song.
2. Sing the song and clap the beat (two beats to a measure). Observe the anacrusis; the first beat is on the first syllable of "*lit*—tle."

3. Sing the song and clap the syllables of the words. This is called clapping the **rhythm pattern.**
4. Sing the song, step the beat, and clap the pattern.

INTRODUCE THE CHART

Note: Use the inquiry method.

Line 1

- What would happen if the drum major did not keep the beat? How does keeping the beat help a parade?
- Point to the illustrations of the drum major and sing "When Johnny Comes Marching Home" while keeping the beat on the chart. Repeat the line as many times as necessary to complete the song.
- Ask a student to keep the beat on the chart while the class sings the song and claps the beat.

Line 2

- If a trapeze artist lost the beat, what would happen?
- Sing "The Man on the Flying Trapeze" while keeping the beat on the chart.

Line 3

- Adapt the above activities for Line 3.

OTHER SONGS TO USE

Line 1

"Yankee Doodle" • "Tramp, Tramp, Tramp" • "The Marine Corps Hymn"

Line 2

"Michael, Row the Boat Ashore" • "Row, Row, Row Your Boat" • "Come Skating with Me."

Line 3

"French Cathedrals" • "Hush, Little Baby" • "Are You Sleeping?"

ADDITIONAL ACTIVITIES

1. Use appropriate instruments with each song, keeping the beat:
   - Line 1: drums, sticks, woodblock
   - Line 2: drum, tambourine, cymbals
   - Line 3: triangle, resonator bells (using *F* and *C* on the beat)

2. Clap the pattern to one of the songs suggested without singing. The student who correctly identifies the song will keep the beat on the correct illustration on the chart while the class sings the song.

3. Choose one student to clap the pattern of a **mystery song** (see list of Musical Terms) for the class to identify and sing. For example,

The lit — tle   bells of West—min—ster . . .

clap clap clap clap clap clap   clap clap

4. Step the pattern while singing one of the songs.

- *Variation:* Divide the class into two groups. Group 1 sings and claps the pattern of the first phrase, and Group 2 sings and steps the pattern of the second phrase.
- If the class has had sufficient preparatory rhythmic experience, perform the above activity without singing the song. Move from phrase to phrase without losing the beat.

5. Sing "The Little Bells of Westminster" as a **round.** Divide the class into two, three, or four groups, and repeat the song three times. Clap or step the song as a round without singing.

EVALUATION OF RHYTHMIC AND PERCEPTUAL SKILLS

Psychomotor Development and Perception

1. Can the students keep the beat with their hands, feet, and body?
2. Is their motion relaxed and free? Do their arms swing freely with the beat of the song (laterality)?
3. Can they turn the phrases while walking or marching the beat without losing their balance or the beat (position in space)?

Aural Acuity and Perception

1. Can the students identify a song by its rhythm pattern?
2. Can they clap a mystery song for the rest of the class to identify?

Visual Acuity and Perception

Can the students follow the figures on the chart while singing, clapping, marching?

Read the Beat

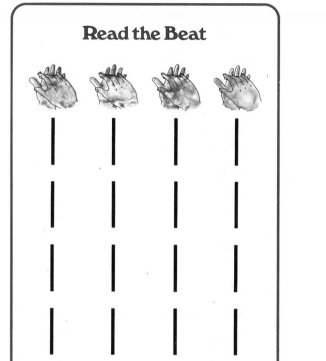

WHY SHOULDN'T MY GOOSE

Traditional Round

1. Why should-n't my goose,

2. Grow as fat as thy goose,

3. When I paid for my goose,

4. Twice as much as thine?

PREPARATION FOR THE CHART

1. Teach the song.
2. Sing the song and clap the beat.
3. Sing the song and step the beat.
4. Sing the song, walk the beat, and turn the phrases.
5. Sing the song, clap the pattern, and step the beat.
6. Sing the song, step the pattern, and clap the beat.

Note: This activity will have to be repeated several times before all the students are successful. Later, combine the above three activities and turn the phrases. This is a highly integrated activity and will require great concentration.

INTRODUCE THE CHART

1. Point to the beats on the chart while the students clap the rhythm symbols. Move from line to line without losing the beat.
2. Clap the pattern of "Why Shouldn't My Goose" as a mystery song for the class to identify.
3. Sing the song and clap the beat while you point to the beats on the chart, moving from line to line without losing the beat.
4. Choose a student to keep the beat on the chart while the class sings the song.
5. Tell the students that the symbols on the chart are called "ta's." They will use this

rhythm syllable every time they read l. For example,

$$\mathsf{l\ \ l\ \ l\ \ l}$$

ta ta ta ta

6. Read the chart with ta's and clap the beat.

OTHER SONGS TO USE

"Marching to Praetoria" • "Upward Trail" • "Are You Sleeping?"

Note: There are innumerable songs that can be used with this chart, but until the students are confident with the beat, avoid songs that have an anacrusis or pick-up.

ADDITIONAL ACTIVITIES

1. Select a song appropriate to the grade level. Use the song as a mystery song by clapping the pattern. The student who correctly identifies the song can be the teacher and keep the beat on the chart while the class sings the song.
2. Choose a familiar song to sing and decide which instrument would be appropriate as an accompaniment. For example,

   "Marching to Praetoria"—drum
   "Upward Trail"—sticks or woodblock
   "Are You Sleeping?"—triangle or
   finger cymbals

3. To encourage musical discrimination, let the students decide which instrument to use.
4. Encourage the students to decide whether the instrumental accompaniment should be loud or soft.

5. Divide the class and sing the song as a two-, three-, or four-part round, repeating the song three or more times.
   - Clap the pattern of the song as a round without singing.
   - Step the pattern of the song as a round without singing.

EVALUATION OF RHYTHMIC AND PERCEPTUAL SKILLS

Psychomotor Development and Perception

1. Do the students step or walk the beat with increasing confidence?
2. Can the students turn the phrases without losing the beat (position in space)?
3. Can the students clap and step the pattern of a song?

Aural and Visual Acuity and Perception

1. Do the students follow the beats on the chart with their eyes?
2. Can the students identify a mystery song when they hear the rhythm pattern?

Musical Development and Social Maturity

1. Can the students choose an appropriate instrument to accompany a song?
2. Can the students decide whether the song or accompaniment should be loud or soft?
3. Do the students contribute to the song by suggesting and volunteering to play an instrumental accompaniment?
4. Do the students participate and sing with enjoyment?

Inner Hearing

PAW PAW PATCH

Kentucky Singing Game

1. Where, oh, where is pret-ty lit-tle Nel - lie?

Where, oh, where is pret-ty lit-tle Nel - lie?

Where, oh, where is pret-ty lit-tle Nel - lie?

Way down yon-der in the paw paw patch.

2. Come on, boys, and let's go find her. *(3 times)*
   Way down yonder in the paw paw patch.
3. Pickin' up paw paws, puttin' in a basket. *(3 times)*
   Way down yonder in the paw paw patch.

PREPARATION FOR THE CHART

1. Teach the song. There are many variations to this song. Change the name to one of the students in the class.
2. Sing the song and clap the beat.
3. Sing the song and step the beat.
4. Sing the song and clap the pattern (words).
5. Sing the song and put the pattern in the feet.
6. Sing the song, clap the pattern, and step or walk the beat.
7. Sing the song, clap the pattern, walk the beat, and turn the phrases.
8. Sing the song, clap "Where, oh, where is" and step "pretty little Nellie." Clap and step "Way down yonder in the paw paw patch."

INTRODUCE THE CHART

1. Discuss the illustrations. What do they mean?

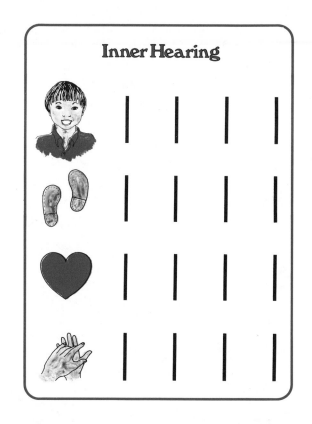

2. Point to the beats on Line 1. Say the ta's.
3. Point to the beats on Line 2. Step the ta's.
4. Explain to the class that the heart means to put the beat inside, and it is therefore silent. Point to the beats on Line 3. Feel the beat.

*Note: From now on, this will be referred to as **inner hearing,** which is an important part of musical training.*

5. Point to the beats on Line 4. Clap the ta's.
6. Clap "Paw Paw Patch" as a mystery song.
7. Sing the song while the teacher points to the beats on the chart.
8. Repeat the song or sing the next verse and follow the directions on the chart: sing Line 1, step Line 2, feel Line 3, and clap Line 4.
9. Vary the order of the chart by starting on Line 2 or Line 3.

10. Choose one of the students to keep the beats on the chart while the class sings the song.

   *Note: In order to establish the **pitch** of the song, it is recommended to begin the chart by singing Line 1 and varying the activities during the other lines. If inner hearing is used on the last phrase of the song, sing the last word of the song together.*

OTHER SONGS TO USE

"Land of the Silver Birch" • "Canoe Song" • "Kookaburra"

Note: Many of the songs for students in the upper grades are longer than the beats presented on the chart. Repeat the chart as many times as necessary to complete the song.

ADDITIONAL ACTIVITIES

1. Make flash cards of the illustrations on the chart:

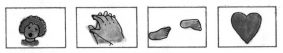

   Select a familiar song to sing. While the class is singing, change the cards at random and follow the directions while keeping the beat. This activity can be expanded to include flash cards of various instruments available to the students. The instruments may play either the beats or the rhythm pattern. When the instrument is playing, the rest of the class is silent.

2. *Radio Game:* Ask the students to describe the motions they would use to turn on a radio. When the radio is turned off, does the music stop at the radio station? The class will soon decide that the music continues, even though the set is turned off. Select a song. Turn the knob of the imaginary radio on and start singing the song. Turn the radio off, but keep the song going inside (inner hearing). Turn the radio back on. Did everyone come in on the same word? Play the game, turning the imaginary radio on and off at random, not necessarily by phrase. Choose different students to operate the radio.

EVALUATION OF RHYTHMIC AND PERCEPTUAL SKILLS

Psychomotor Development and Perception

1. Can the children move from one activity to another without losing the beat?
2. Can the students play an instrument while reading the chart?

Aural Acuity and Perception

1. Can the students feel the beat with inner hearing?
2. Can they sing a song with inner hearing and not lose the beat or melody?

Visual Acuity and Perception

1. Do the children read the symbols on the chart and move from line to line without losing the beat?
2. Can the students follow visual directions and keep the beat?

Musical Development and Social Maturity

1. Are the students becoming increasingly aware of the beat of a song?
2. Are the students becoming increasingly aware of phrases of a song?

Phrasing

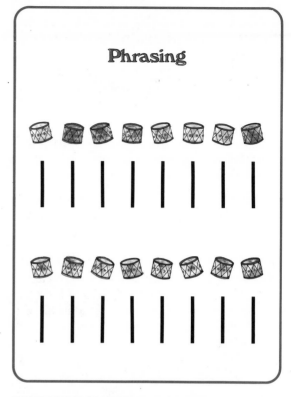

Phrasing

YANKEE DOODLE

Traditional

Yank - ee Doo - dle went to town a - rid - ing on a po — ny,

Stuck a feath - er in his cap and called it mac - a - ro — ni.

Refrain

Yank - ee Doo - dle, keep it up, Yank - ee Doo - dle dan - dy,

Mind the mu - sic and the step, And with the girls be han - dy.

PREPARATION FOR THE CHART

1. Teach the song.
2. Sing the song and clap the beat.
3. Sing the song and step or walk the beat.
4. Sing the song and clap the pattern.
5. Sing the song and step the pattern.
6. Sing the song, step the pattern, and clap the beat.

INTRODUCE THE CHART

1. Ask the students what the song says first. *"Yankee Doodle went to town a—riding on a pony"* This is the first phrase (⌢).
2. Point to the chart (to either the illustrations or the rhythm symbols) and sing the first phrase.
3. Point to the chart and sing the second phrase. Continue through the entire song, phrase by phrase.

19

4. Point to the beats, saying and clapping the ta's (I). How many beats are there in each phrase? *8*
5. Point to the beats on the chart, sing the song, and make large arm movements for each phrase—first with the right arm, then with the left arm.

Note: Tell the students they are making the motion for a phrase. *Add this word to their musical vocabulary.*

6. Choose one student to keep the beat on the chart while the class sings the song. Be sure to keep the beat while going from phrase to phrase.
7. Sing the song and tap the ta's on the chart. While the class is singing, tap the beats for the first phrase with the fingers of the right hand and the beats for the second phrase with the knuckles of the left hand. Repeat for Phrases 3 and 4.
8. Point to the beats on the chart, sing "Yankee Doodle," then put the song inside (inner hearing). Follow the beats through the song, and all sing "macaroni" together. Repeat this activity for Phrases 3 and 4.
9. This last activity can be varied by singing the first and last word of each phrase and clapping or stepping the beat or pattern for inner hearing.

OTHER SONGS TO USE

"Who Did?" • "I've Been to Haarlem" • "Hush, Little Baby"

Note: Let the students decide where the phrases occur. Some songs may have four beats to a phrase and some may have eight or more beats to a phrase. Encourage the students to decide whether the phrases are identical or different (A–B, A–B–A, A–A–B, and so on). This is the beginning of understanding **form** *in music.*

ADDITIONAL ACTIVITIES

1. Choose a familiar song to sing and decide where the phrases occur. While singing the song, make the phrase marks on a large piece of paper.

Note: The tendency of students when beginning this activity is to make the first phrase from left to right and the second phrase from right to left:

While this is acceptable, it does not follow the pattern of musical notation or the printed page. Encourage the students to make all phrase markings from left to right:

Some songs will have more than two phrases. Let the students discover this and decide how many phrases there are in the song.

2. Select a song to sing and while singing mark the beats on a large piece of paper or on the chalkboard. The beats (I) should be by phrases in four or eight beats:

Are you sleep—ing? Are you sleep—ing?
I I I   I I I I.   I

Who did, who did? Who did, who did?
I   I   I   I

3. Sing the song, step the beat, and turn the phrase (change direction) without losing the beat.
4. Divide the class into two groups. Form two lines facing each other, but spaced so that the students are not directly opposite each other. The first group walks the beat forward on the first phrase, while the second group walks the beat forward on the second phrase. The lines will pass through (this is a preparation for folkdancing). If there are more than two phrases, also walk the beat backward.

EVALUATION OF RHYTHMIC AND PERCEPTUAL SKILLS

Psychomotor Development and Perception

1. Can the students change direction and keep the beat (position in space)?
2. Can they change from gross motor activity to a fine motor activity, for example, walking the beat for one phrase then tapping the beat for the second phrase?

Aural and Visual Acuity and Perception

1. Can the students sing the song and recognize the phrase?
2. Can the students match the beats on the chart to the song?

Musical Development and Social Maturity

1. Do the students have an increasing awareness of musical form? Can they identify:
   - identical phrases: A–A?
   - phrases that are different: A–B?
   - repetition: A–B–A?
2. Is there an increasing spontaneity while singing a song?
3. Do the students volunteer to lead the class?
4. Do they listen to others and follow directions?

The Rest

The Rest

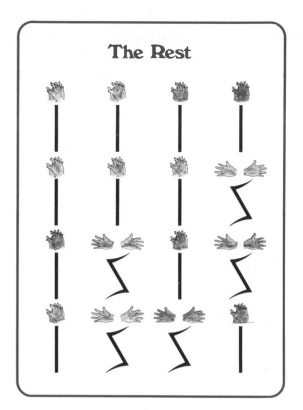

PREPARATION FOR THE CHART

The **quarter rest** (𝄽) is silent but has a beat. Clap the beats (I—ta) and throw the rest away:

The rest is the rhythm symbol for silence, but the beat continues.

INTRODUCE THE CHART

1. Select one student to read and clap the first line of the chart.
2. What does the class see at the end of the second line? 𝄽 Tell the students that this is the symbol or sign for a rest. The beat is silent, and they are to make the rest motion by throwing their hands out and feeling the silent beat.

3. Select individuals in the class to read and clap one line of the chart while you point to the beats on the chart.
4. Read and clap the entire chart without losing the beat, saying the ta's and feeling the rest.
5. Sing "Hush, Little Baby" and read and clap the first two lines of the chart.

Note: These two lines are repeated four times for the first verse of the song.

6. Choose one student to point to the rhythm symbols on the chart while the class claps the rhythm pattern and sings "Marching to Praetoria."
7. Sing "Are You Sleeping?" and read and clap Line 4 of the chart through the entire song.

Point to the rhythm symbols on the chart while the class sings the song:

$$I \cdot \quad 𝄽 \quad 𝄽 \quad I$$

8. Select a familiar song. Step the beat and read and clap the entire chart, moving from line to line without losing the beat. The chart will probably have to be repeated several times for the complete song. Choose one of the students to lead the class by keeping the beat and pointing to the rhythm symbols on the chart.

OTHER SONGS TO USE

- "In Bahía"—maracas or claves *(clah–vehs)*
- "Hush, Little Baby"—triangle or finger cymbals
- "Upward Trail"—drum or sticks

Note: This chart can be used in many different ways, depending upon the maturity of your class. Play the rhythm symbols on an appropriate instrument, using either one line of the chart or the entire chart as an accompaniment.

ADDITIONAL ACTIVITIES

1. Clap variations and have the class echo with ta's and clapping, making the motion for the rest (echo clapping).

Teacher or leader claps	Class says and claps (on the beat)
❘ ❘ ❘ 𝄽	ta ta ta rest
❘ 𝄽 ❘ 𝄽	ta rest ta rest
❘ 𝄽 𝄽 ❘	ta rest rest ta
𝄽 𝄽 ❘ ❘	rest rest ta ta

2. *Dictation:* The students will write the patterns after they clap and say them.

Note: The quarter rest is made by slanting the ta (\ ), then adding an arm (⌐) and a leg (⌐). Have the students practice making the rest on the chalkboard or paper to give them confidence.

Teacher claps	Class says and claps	Class writes
❘ ❘ ❘ 𝄽	ta ta ta rest	❘ ❘ ❘ 𝄽
❘ 𝄽 ❘ 𝄽	ta rest ta rest	❘ 𝄽 ❘ 𝄽
𝄽 𝄽 𝄽 ❘	rest rest rest ta	𝄽 𝄽 𝄽 ❘

3. Make flash cards of various rhythm patterns:

❘ 𝄽 ❘ 𝄽	❘ ❘ ❘ 𝄽	❘ ❘ 𝄽 𝄽

Show one card. The class responds by clapping and saying the ta's. Try to keep the beat while going from card to card. This activity can be done with individual students, moving from one to the other without losing the beat.

4. *Mirror Image and Echo Clapping:* Clap pattern variations creating different tone qualities, for example, knuckles on desk, patting knees, fingers on book, and so on. Move from pattern to pattern without losing the beat. The class repeats (echoes) the pattern given by the leader.

5. Choose a familiar song. Decide on a pattern to clap throughout the entire song. The students will be more successful at this activity if the pattern is put on the chalkboard.

6. Sing a familiar song. Have several students play a pattern (for example, ❘ 𝄽 ❘ ❘) on a rhythm instrument to accompany the song. This pattern is called an **ostinato.**

Note: Tell the class the word ostinato is Italian and means stubborn, so they must hold on to the pattern. Add this word to their musical vocabulary.

7. Select individuals to lead the class in echo clapping and mirror image using variations of a pattern. When the leader loses the beat, he or she sits down and another student becomes the leader.

EVALUATION OF RHYTHMIC AND PERCEPTUAL SKILLS

Psychomotor Development and Perception

1. Can the students echo a given pattern without losing the beat?
2. Can the students write a dictated pattern containing rests?

Aural Acuity and Perception

1. Can the students recognize and read the rest as a silent beat?
2. Can the students maintain an ostinato while a song is being sung?

6
Old MacDonald

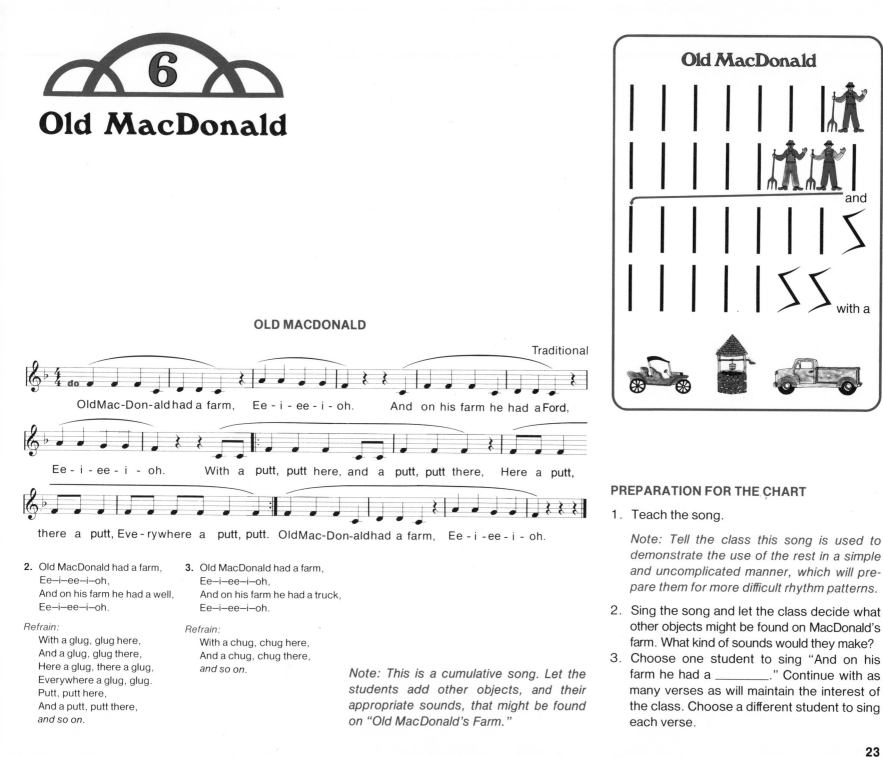

OLD MACDONALD

Traditional

do

Old Mac-Don-ald had a farm, Ee - i - ee - i - oh. And on his farm he had a Ford,

Ee - i - ee - i - oh. With a putt, putt here, and a putt, putt there, Here a putt,

there a putt, Eve-ry where a putt, putt. Old Mac-Don-ald had a farm, Ee - i - ee - i - oh.

2. Old MacDonald had a farm,
Ee–i–ee–i–oh,
And on his farm he had a well,
Ee–i–ee–i–oh.

Refrain:
With a glug, glug here,
And a glug, glug there,
Here a glug, there a glug,
Everywhere a glug, glug.
Putt, putt here,
And a putt, putt there,
and so on.

3. Old MacDonald had a farm,
Ee–i–ee–i–oh,
And on his farm he had a truck,
Ee–i–ee–i–oh.

Refrain:
With a chug, chug here,
And a chug, chug there,
and so on.

Note: This is a cumulative song. Let the students add other objects, and their appropriate sounds, that might be found on "Old MacDonald's Farm."

Old MacDonald

and

with a

PREPARATION FOR THE CHART

1. Teach the song.

   Note: Tell the class this song is used to demonstrate the use of the rest in a simple and uncomplicated manner, which will prepare them for more difficult rhythm patterns.

2. Sing the song and let the class decide what other objects might be found on MacDonald's farm. What kind of sounds would they make?

3. Choose one student to sing "And on his farm he had a _____." Continue with as many verses as will maintain the interest of the class. Choose a different student to sing each verse.

INTRODUCE THE CHART

1. Read the pattern with clapping and ta's. Make the motion for the rest and feel the beat.
2. Point to the pattern on the chart and sing the song, keeping the beat. Clap the beat for the refrain of the song.
3. Select one student to be the leader, who should point to the rhythm symbols on the chart while the class sings the song. Each leader will decide the subject and the appropriate sound for the verse they lead.
4. Point to the pattern on the chart, sing the song, and dramatize the subject; for example, while singing "glug, glug," pump the handle up and down.

ADDITIONAL ACTIVITIES

1. Sing the song without the chart and have the students write the pattern on the chalkboard or a piece of paper (verse only).
2. Sing the song, walk the beat (remember, the rest gets a beat), and turn the phrases. Continue walking the beat for the refrain, but dramatize each subject with arm or body motions.
3. Sing the song, but clap and do not sing the sound effects of each verse. Be sure to keep the beat while singing the song.
4. Sing the song and have one group of students play a pattern on rhythm instruments (ostinato).

5. Sing the song while seated:

   - First beat—slap knees
   - Second beat—clap
   - Third beat—snap fingers of both hands
   - Fourth beat—clap

   Continue this activity through the entire song.

6. Use variations of the above activity.

   - Sing the first phrase using the above activity, and step the second phrase. Continue throughout the song.
   - Sit in a circle in groups of four. Sing the song. On the first beat, slap knees; on the second beat, clap own hands; third beat, clap hands of the persons sitting on each side; fourth beat, clap own hands. Keeping the beat while singing the song will improve peripheral vision.

7. Assign a rhythm instrument to individual students. Sing the song and play the pattern of the sound.

EVALUATION OF RHYTHMIC AND PERCEPTUAL SKILLS

Visual Acuity and Perception

1. Can the students read and follow the pattern on the chart, moving from line to line?
2. Can the students clap hands with their partner's to each side, using peripheral vision without losing the beat?

I Can Play

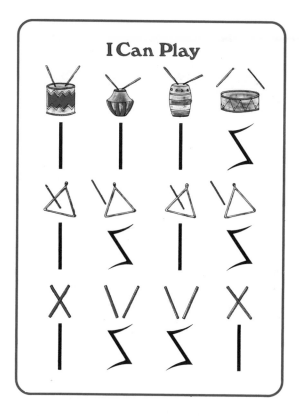

The use of instruments involves a more integrated set of motions combining singing, reading of symbols on the chart, and fine motor skills. This involvement will have a direct relationship to learning activities in other areas of the curriculum. Use this chart many times with familiar songs and favorite recordings. Encourage the students to use musical discrimination and to become aware of loud and soft; for example:

- Drum—loud: "Yankee Doodle"
- Triangle—soft: "Are You Sleeping?"
- Claves—medium loud: "In Bahía"

The students should be ready to expand their musical vocabulary. Introduce these musical terms:

p—*piano:* soft (*piano* means *soft* in Italian)
pp—*pianissimo:* very soft
mp—*mezzo piano:* medium soft (*mezzo* means *half* or *middle* in Italian)
f—*forte:* loud (*forte* means *loud* in Italian)
mf—*mezzo forte:* medium loud
ff—*fortissimo:* very loud

PREPARATION FOR THE CHART

1. Introduce the instruments shown on the chart.
2. Clap the pattern of a familiar song without singing. Let the class guess the name of the song (mystery song). Sing the song and clap the pattern.
3. Ask the students which instrument on the chart would sound best as an accompaniment to the song. Should the song be sung softly (*p*) or vigorously (*f*)? (Loud does not mean to shout.) For example:

   - "Marching to Praetoria": drum—forte (loud)
   - "Hush, Little Baby": triangle—piano (soft)
   - "Angelique-O": claves—mezzo forte (medium loud)

INTRODUCE THE CHART

1. Point to the first line of the chart. What sound does the drum make? *boom* Dramatize playing the drum on Line 1, say "boom," and make the sign for the rest. Is a drum loud or soft?

2. Continue through Line 2 and Line 3 of the chart, saying "ting" for the triangle and "click" for the claves.
3. Read the illustrations on the chart without losing the beat. Make the sound of the instrument and dramatize playing it as you read the chart.

Note: Encourage the students to change their voices to fit the instrument, from the deep sound of the drum to the high, thin sound of the triangle and the sharp sound of the claves.

4. Select one student to be the leader and point to the rhythm symbols (I, ⸘) on the chart while the class claps and says the rhythm syllables and makes the sign for the rest.

5. Select a familiar song and clap one line of the chart as an ostinato while a student keeps the beat on the chart. As the class becomes more confident, clap the entire chart as an accompaniment.

OTHER SONGS TO USE

Drum

"Marching to Praetoria" • "Upward Trail" • "Land of the Silver Birch"

Triangle

"Au Clair de la Lune" • "Hush, Little Baby" • "Ah, Poor Bird"

Claves

"Old Brass Wagon" • "Chairs to Mend" • "Donkey Riding"

ADDITIONAL ACTIVITIES

1. Make a large classroom chart with drawings or pictures of the instruments available to the class. Let the students decide what words describe the sound each instrument makes. Put the pictures on the left of the chart and their sound on the right:

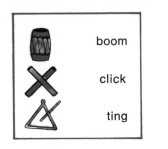

Select a song and divide the class. Have one group sing the song while the other group dramatizes playing and makes the sound of the instrument that you point to on the chart. Skip from one illustration to another without losing the beat.

2. Select a song. Divide the class into several groups. Pass out the various instruments pictured on the chart. Choose a leader to point to the instruments on the chart while the class sings the song. The leader may change the instrument whenever she or he chooses, and the class must be ready to keep the beat and play only when it is their turn.

3. Make flash cards of various patterns using ta's and rests:

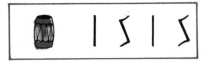

As you show each card, those students having the instrument on the card must play the pattern. When the class becomes more confident, you can use the cards as an instrumental accompaniment to a song.

EVALUATION OF RHYTHMIC AND PERCEPTUAL SKILLS

Psychomotor Development and Perception

1. Can the students play an instrument and sing a song simultaneously?
2. Can the students play an instrument and keep the beat?

Aural and Visual Acuity and Perception

1. Do the students show increasing awareness of the appropriate sounds to accompany a song?
2. Do the students look at the charts or flash cards and read the correct pattern and play the instrument pictured?

Anacrusis

SHE'LL BE COMIN' 'ROUND THE MOUNTAIN

Southern Mountain Song

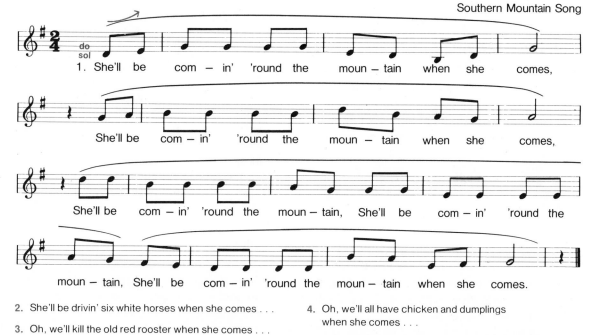

1. She'll be com — in' 'round the moun — tain when she comes,

She'll be com — in' 'round the moun — tain when she comes,

She'll be com — in' 'round the moun — tain, She'll be com — in' 'round the

moun — tain, She'll be com — in' 'round the moun — tain when she comes.

2. She'll be drivin' six white horses when she comes . . .

3. Oh, we'll kill the old red rooster when she comes . . .

4. Oh, we'll all have chicken and dumplings when she comes . . .

5. Oh, we'll all go out to meet her when she comes . . .

Note: Many of the songs that young people sing have an anacrusis or pick-up. This simply means that a song does not start on the first beat of the measure, but on the up-beat or a portion of the preceding measure. This will naturally put the accent on the first beat of the following measure. Several familiar examples are given below:

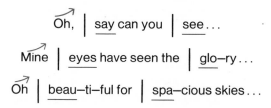

Oh, | say can you | see . . .

Mine | eyes have seen the | glo—ry . . .

Oh | beau—ti—ful for | spa—cious skies . . .

Introduce the word anacrusis *to the class. They will enjoy using it, and it should become a part of their musical vocabulary.*

PREPARATION FOR THE CHART

1. Teach the song, using as many verses as will maintain the interest of the class.
2. Sing the song and clap the beat. To make the motion for the anacrusis, extend both arms to the side and clap the first beat:

She'll be | com—in'

3. Sing the song and clap the pattern. Use the motion for the anacrusis, and accent the first beat:

She'll be | com—in' 'round the |

moun—tain . . .

4. Sing the song, step the beat, clap the pattern, and make the motion for the anacrusis.
5. Sing the song, step the beat, and clap only the first beat of each measure (accent—see list of Musical Terms).
6. Sing the song, clap the beat, and step the pattern.
7. All sing "She'll be comin' " and then put the song inside (inner hearing) until the last word of the phrase "comes." Continue through the entire song.
8. Choose a leader to clap the pattern as a mystery song.

INTRODUCE THE CHART

1. Point to the rhythm symbols on the chart while the class reads and claps the pattern.
2. Select one student to read and clap the chart with rhythm syllables (ta's).
3. Ask the class what the arrow means on the chart *anacrusis or pick-up*

4. Sing "She'll Be Comin' 'Round the Mountain," using the motion for the anacrusis and clapping the chart while singing the song.

   Note: The chart will have to be repeated to sing the entire song. Move from the bottom of the chart to the first ta at the top without losing the beat.

5. Choose one student to lead the class by pointing to the rhythm symbols on the chart while the class sings the song. Make the motion for the anacrusis with one hand and keep the beat on the chart.

OTHER SONGS TO USE

- "Polly Wolly Doodle":
  Oh, I | went down south . . .

- "Erie Canal":
  I | got a mule . . .

- "When the Saints Go Marching" (refrain):
  Oh, when the | saints . . .

ADDITIONAL ACTIVITIES

1. Teach the dance to "She'll Be Comin' 'Round the Mountain." Form a large circle with sets of two couples facing each other. The facing couples should be far enough apart so that they can take four steps toward each other.

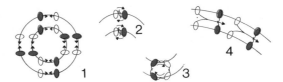

- *Phrase 1:* The couples, with hands joined beginning on the first beat step or skip forward toward the facing couple (four beats), bow slightly, and skip back to place (four beats).
- *Phrase 2:* Facing couples again skip forward. Each dancer links arms with the

person opposite, swings around once, and skips back to place.
- *Phrase 3:* Facing couples join hands and circle left until each couple is back in place.
- *Phrase 4:* One of the couples skips through an arch formed by the arms of the other couple, so that each couple is now facing a new couple.

Repeat the dance as often as desired. Keep the beat by walking or skipping.

2. Select several students to read and play the rhythm pattern of the chart on classroom instruments while the class sings a familiar song.

- *Variation:* Choose four students to play an instrument, reading only one line of the chart while the class sings the song; for example, Line 1—wood block; Line 2—sticks; Line 3—drum; Line 4—tambourine.

EVALUATION OF RHYTHMIC AND PERCEPTUAL SKILLS

Psychomotor Development and Perception

1. Can the students, through motor activities, feel the accent of the song?
2. Can the students read the chart and play an instrument while the class is singing a familiar song?
3. Are the students becoming increasingly confident while performing integrated activities?

Aural and Visual Acuity and Perception

1. Are the students becoming increasingly confident with rhythm patterns using the silent beat (rest)?
2. Can the students read a chart using ta's and rests?

Rhythms

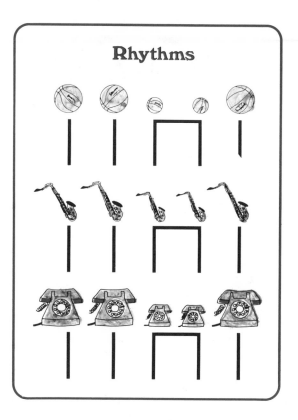

Note: Charts 9, 10, and 11 teach the same basic concept, and therefore the "Evaluation of Rhythmic and Perceptual Skills" appears at the end of Chart 11.

PREPARATION FOR THE CHART

Note: In the preceding charts, the rhythm pattern was a combination of beats and rests (|, 𝄽). Now, we have a new symbol (⊓), which has two sounds to the beat (ti–ti), but has the same duration as ta (|). Ta (|) is a **quarter note** (♩) and ti–ti (⊓) is two **eighth notes** (♪♪).

1. Ask individuals to clap the pattern of their name (syllabication).

Kath–leen Fla–her–ty: | | ⊓ |
Mich–ael Con–nal–ly: | | ⊓ |
Mar–y Ann Ber–go–vich: ⊓ | ⊓ |

INTRODUCE THE CHART

1. Point to the illustrations on the chart and clap the pattern of the words:

   • Line 1: Ball, ball, bas–ket–ball
   • Line 2: Sax, sax, sax–o–phone
   • Line 3: Phone, phone, tel–e–phone

2. Point to the illustrations on the chart and say and step the pattern of the words.

3. Point to the rhythm pattern on the chart. Is there something new? Tell the class that when they see ⊓ they should read "ti–ti."

4. Point to the rhythm symbols and read and clap the entire chart with ta's and ti's. (Do not point to each small figure, only the first one of the pair, for that is where the beat is felt.)

5. Select individual students to read and clap the rhythm symbols of one line of the chart while you keep the beat.

6. Select a leader to keep the beat on the chart while the class reads and claps the rhythm symbols.

7. Proceed to the next chart.

More Rhythms

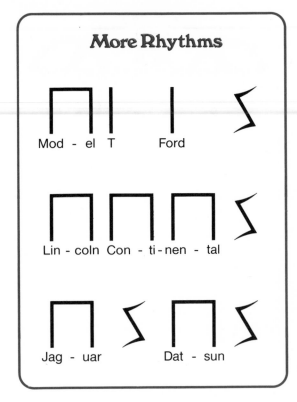

More Rhythms

Mod - el T   Ford

Lin - coln Con - ti - nen - tal

Jag - uar   Dat - sun

INTRODUCE THE CHART

1. Ask for volunteers to read and clap one line of the chart, using the words (syllabication).
2. Read and clap the entire chart using the words and moving from line to line without losing the beat.
3. Read and clap the entire chart with rhythm syllables (ta's and ti's).
4. Select a leader to keep the beat on the chart while the class reads and claps the rhythm symbols.
5. Divide the class into three groups. Assign one line of the chart to each group, using a different sound for each line. For example, have the group assigned to Line 1 clap; Line 2, rap their knuckles on their desks; Line 3, tap their books. Point to the rhythm symbols on the chart, keeping the beat while each groups reads its pattern.

Note: As the students become more confident and proficient, they will be able to do the above activity without a leader. This involves feeling the beat and using visual perception to interpret the symbols on the chart.

OTHER SONGS TO USE

Use one line of the chart as an ostinato or the entire chart as a rhythmic accompaniment to a familiar song. This may be done with clapping, stepping, tapping, or playing a classroom instrument. Encourage the students to exercise musical discrimination in their choice of dynamics and type of instrumentation.

- "Battle Hymn of the Republic" (refrain): drum—forte
- "Sourwood Mountain": tambourine—mezzo forte
- "The Little Bells of Westminster": triangle or finger cymbals—piano

ADDITIONAL ACTIVITIES

1. Starting with Chart 7, move from chart to chart without losing the beat, using previous rhythmic experiences. Practice:

- clapping
- stepping
- tapping
- playing instruments
- inner hearing

2. Clap a pattern using ta's, ti's, and rests. The class echoes the clapped pattern and then speaks the rhythm syllables. Use many different variations of patterns.

Leader claps   Class claps

Class speaks

ta   ti–ti ta   ta
ti–ti ta   ti–ti ta
ta   rest ti–ti ta

The patterns can be as difficult as the class is capable of doing.

3. Proceed to the next chart.

Mystery Songs

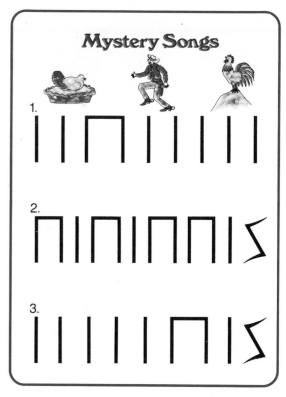

Mystery Songs

1.

2.

3.

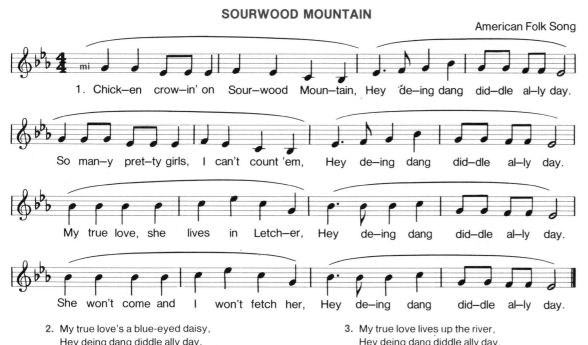

SOURWOOD MOUNTAIN

American Folk Song

mi

1. Chick—en crow—in' on Sour—wood Moun—tain, Hey 'de—ing dang did—dle al—ly day.

So man—y pret—ty girls, I can't count 'em, Hey de—ing dang did—dle al—ly day.

My true love, she lives in Letch—er, Hey de—ing dang did—dle al—ly day.

She won't come and I won't fetch her, Hey de—ing dang did—dle al—ly day.

2. My true love's a blue-eyed daisy,
   Hey deing dang diddle ally day.
   If I don't get her, I'll go crazy,
   Hey deing dang diddle ally day.
   Big dog bark and little one bite you,
   Hey deing dang diddle ally day.
   Big girl court and little one slight you
   Hey deing dang diddle ally day.

3. My true love lives up the river,
   Hey deing dang diddle ally day.
   A few more jumps and I'll be with her,
   Hey deing dang diddle ally day.
   My true love lives up the holler,
   Hey deing dang diddle ally day.
   She won't come and I won't foller,
   Hey deing dang diddle ally day.

PREPARATION FOR THE CHART

Note: This chart is a continuation of the preceding two charts and is based on previous learnings. The use of various combinations of rhythm symbols will provide a greater variety of rhythmic experiences and contribute to the student's confidence in the psychomotor domain.

1. Teach the songs.
2. Sing the songs and use previous rhythmic experiences:

   - Clap the beat
   - Clap the pattern
   - Step the beat and clap the pattern
   - Combine these activities
   - Walk the beat and turn the phrases
   - Use the rhythm patterns as a mystery song
   - Practice inner hearing

OLD JOE CLARK

American Folk Song

Old Joe Clark he had a house Six—teen sto—ries high; Ev—ery sto—ry

Refrain

in that house Was filled with chick—en pie. 'Round and 'round, Old Joe Clark,

'Round and 'round I say; 'Round and 'round, Old Joe Clark, I have—n't long to stay.

SKIP TO MY LOU

American Folk Song

1. Lost my part—ner, what will I do? Lost my part—ner, what will I do? Lost my part—ner

Refrain

what will I do? Skip to my Lou, my dar — ling. Lou, Lou, skip to my Lou, Lou, Lou,

skip to my Lou, Lou, Lou, skip to my Lou, Skip to my Lou, my dar — ling.

2. I'll get another one, pretty as you, *(3 times)*
Skip to my Lou, my darling.

3. Little red wagon, painted blue, *(3 times)*
Skip to my Lou, my darling.

4. Flies in the sugar bowl, shoo, fly, shoo, *(3 times)*
Skip to my Lou, my darling.

INTRODUCE THE CHART

Note: These are song fragments from the above songs using a familiar rhythm pattern. The pattern for "Old Joe Clark" is the beginning of the refrain. Be sure the class is familiar with the songs before you introduce the chart.

1. This chart can be used as a game. Clap one of the rhythm patterns on the chart, and have the class identify which one was clapped by raising one finger for Line 1, two fingers for Line 2, and three fingers for Line 3.

2. Clap one of the rhythm patterns on the chart. The student who correctly identifies

the song may lead the class while they sing the song (mystery song). If the student is confident, he or she may wish to sing the song as a solo. This should be a volunteer activity.

3. Choose one student to keep the beat on the chart while the class claps the pattern and reads the ta's and ti's, moving from line to line without losing the beat.

4. Select a familiar song to sing, and use one line on the chart as a rhythmic ostinato with clapping or stepping.

5. For the musically capable class, try using all three lines of the chart as an ostinato. Start the first ostinato to establish the beat, then add the second ostinato, and finally the third. Begin to sing the song. As the class becomes more confident, all parts can begin simultaneously; for example, the song "Marching to Praetoria" could be used in this way:

- First instrument: woodblock
- Second instrument: tambourine
- Third instrument: triangle or finger cymbals
- Class sings the song.

OTHER SONGS TO USE

- "By the Singing Water"
ta ta ta ta ti-ti ti-ti ta ta

- "Come Follow"
ta ti-ti ti-ti ti-ti ti-ti ti-ti ti-ti ta

- "Why Shouldn't My Goose?"
ta ti-ti ta ta ti-ti ti-ti ta ta

ADDITIONAL ACTIVITIES

1. *Echo Clapping and Dictation:*

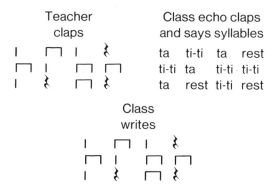

Teacher claps	Class echo claps and says syllables
	ta ti-ti ta rest
	ti-ti ta ti-ti ti-ti
	ta rest ti-ti rest

Class writes

Note: Be sure to make the motion for the rest when clapping the rhythm pattern.

2. *Echo Clapping with Mirror Image:* Remember to keep the beat when moving from one rhythm pattern to another.

Teacher or leader

clap
slap knees
tap desk

Class echoes

clap
slap knees
tap desk

Note: Try to have a different tone quality for each rhythm pattern.

3. Make flash cards of different rhythm patterns. For example:

At first, use the flash cards with the class and later with individuals.

4. Ask for volunteers to clap the pattern of a mystery song for the class to identify. Once the song has been identified, the student who volunteered may lead the class while they sing the entire song. This activity will contribute a great deal to an increased musical repertoire and enable many students to perform in a leadership role.

EVALUATION OF RHYTHMIC AND PERCEPTUAL SKILLS

Psychomotor Development and Perception

Is the class developing the ability to co-ordinate more than one activity, such as clapping a pattern and stepping a beat, eye-hand coordination, or reading a chart and playing an instrument, while using diverse patterns?

Aural Acuity and Perception

1. Can the students hear the silent beat (𝄽)?
2. Can the students hear long and short sounds (।, ⊓)?
3. Can the students identify familiar patterns (mystery songs)?

Visual Acuity and Perception

1. Are the students becoming increasingly confident while reading rhythm symbols on the chart?
2. Can the students identify long and short sounds visually?
3. Can their eyes follow the pattern on the chart, moving from line to line and chart to chart without losing the beat?

Ostinato

Ostinato

‖: | | :‖

Keep   cool.

‖: ⊓ | :‖

Sim - mer   down.

Ostinato

‖: ⊓ ⊓ | ⊓ ⊓ :‖

Worry, worry. | Worry, worry.

---

*Note: This chart is a speaking–rhythm chart in two parts. The symbols are the same. The variety in a spoken rhythm is introduced by the manner in which the voice is used, providing tone color through the use of **dynamics.** The "Evaluation of Rhythmic and Perceptual Skills" is combined with that of Chart 13.*

PREPARATION FOR THE CHART

1. Create verbal story pictures and let the students decide how they would say the following:

   - Fire! Fire! *loudly, with intensity (ff)*
   - Go to sleep *softly, tenderly (pp)*
   - Here, kitty, kitty *gently (mp)*

2. Would they use a loud voice or a soft voice? Would they be excited or calm?

INTRODUCE THE CHART

1. Ask individual students to read and clap the rhythm symbols of each line of the chart.
2. Is there something new on the chart? *repeat signs:* ‖: :‖
3. Tell the class that the double bar with two dots is a **repeat sign.** Everytime they see this sign it means they must repeat what they have just sung or played, either from the beginning of the song or back to the first repeat sign (‖:).
4. Review the meaning of *ostinato* with the class (see the list of Musical Terms).
5. How would the students use their voices to say "Keep cool" *calm and low (mp)*
6. How would they say "Simmer down"? *a little louder with voices sharply accented (mf)*

7. How would the students say "worry, worry, worry, worry"? This chart can be developed into a dramatic story of a disagreement at school and the fear and apprehension at being caught for misbehaving (worry, worry).
8. Divide the class into two groups. Group 1 says "Keep cool" and "Simmer down" with repeats, changing their voices to provide contrast. Those in Group 2 are the "worriers" (ostinato).

Note: When introducing this activity, establish the beat with the ostinato (Group 2), then have Group 1 enter with "Keep cool" and "Simmer down." When the students become more confident, Group 1 and Group 2 can begin at the same time. Establish the beat before the class begins to read the chart.

OTHER MATERIAL TO USE

Create original rhythm patterns from the student's language experiences, such as original stories, reading, and individual experiences. Here are some examples.

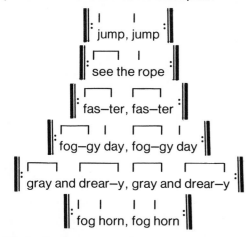

The ostinato can be decided by the teacher or leader. Let the class decide whether their voices should be loud or soft, calm or excited, and so on.

ADDITIONAL ACTIVITIES

1. Divide the class into two groups and read the chart with sound differentiation.

Group 1:
   rapping desk

Group 2:
   clapping

Group 1:
   tapping pencils

Group 2:
   rapping book

This activity can also be done with classroom instruments.

2. Put an extended pattern on the board with repeat bars. The length of the pattern should depend on the maturity of the class.

Read and clap the pattern. Put an ostinato on the board directly under the first pattern. Read and rap (knuckles on book or desk) the pattern.

Divide the class and read both parts. Select individuals to read and clap the patterns simultaneously. Select individuals to play both parts on different sounding instruments.

3. The last activity can be developed into a highly integrated lesson, as is shown in the next chart. You will find many other songs that can be developed in the same manner. Begin with simple and familiar songs and let the class decide what pattern to use as an ostinato.

4. Proceed to the next chart.

Scotland's Burning

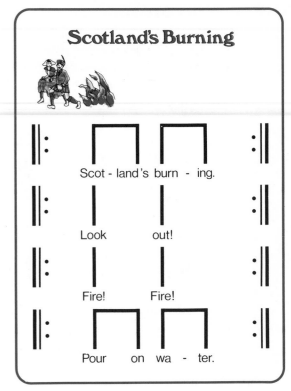

PREPARATION FOR THE CHART

1. Teach the song.
2. Sing the song, using previous rhythmic experiences (see Chart 11).

INTRODUCE THE CHART

1. Read the words with the class, using the repeat bars.
2. Teacher sings the first measure, class sings the repeat without losing the beat (echo).
3. Continue this activity throughout the entire chart without losing the beat.
4. Sing the entire song, starting softly (*piano, p*), building up to "Fire! Fire!" (*forte, f*), and getting softer on "Pour on water" (*mezzo piano, mp*).
5. If the students are familiar with dynamic markings (*p, f*), you might introduce **crescendo** (gradually getting louder) and **decrescendo** (gradually getting softer). The musical symbols for these terms are:

crescendo $<$ decrescendo $>$

Note: These can be related to the mathematical symbols greater than ($<$) and less than ($>$).

6. Select one line of the song to be an ostinato. Divide the class. Have Group 1 start the ostinato and establish the beat. Then have Group 2 begin singing the song, coming in on the beat.

Note: When introducing this activity, it is recommended that you point to the rhythm symbols of the ostinato selected on the chart.

As the class becomes more confident, divide the class into five groups. Have one group sing the song while the other four are ostinatos. Encourage the students to follow the words and rhythm symbols on the chart with their eyes while singing. Suggest that their voices must fit the words in tone color and volume (loud and soft).

OTHER SONGS TO USE

"Are You Sleeping?" • "Canoe Song" • "Down in the Valley"

ADDITIONAL ACTIVITIES

Form

1. Sing the song and dramatize the **melodic contour.** Does the melody start high or low? *low* Does the melody move up or down? *up*

"Scotland's burning" ↗ ↗

SCOTLAND'S BURNING

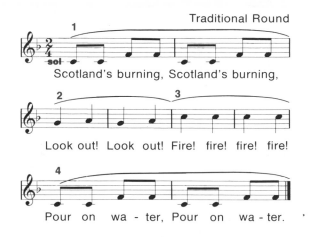

Traditional Round

Scotland's burning, Scotland's burning,

Look out! Look out! Fire! fire! fire! fire!

Pour on wa - ter, Pour on wa - ter.

What happens when we sing "Look out!"?
the melody moves upward slightly

"Look out!"

Is "Fire! Fire!" high or low? *high* Does "Fire! Fire! move at all? *no*

"Fire! Fire!"

Does the melody for "Pour on water" sound familiar? *It's the same as the first phrase, "Scotland's burning."*

"Pour on water"

2. Draw a picture of the melody in the air with large arm movements. Then have the students put the melodic contour on the chalkboard or on a piece of paper in the same fashion. Sing the song while making a picture of the melody. There will be many variations. Accept those that give a conceptual approach to melodic contour.

"Scotland's burning"
"Look out!"
"Fire! Fire!"
"Pour on water."

3. Give letter names to each phrase. If two phrases are alike, give them the same letter (musical form):

"Scotland's burning"—A
"Look out!"—B
"Fire! Fire!"—C
"Pour on water"—A

4. Use the last activity on musical form with other familiar songs. You will find a direct relationship to language development in such areas as

• phrasing
• sequence
• similarities/differences
• visual and aural perception

Instruments

1. Read the chart and play each phrase on a different instrument.

A "Scotland's burning"—sticks and/or woodblocks
B "Look out!"—tambourines or finger cymbals
C "Fire! Fire!"—cymbals or drum
A "Pour on water"—sticks or woodblock

The same instrumentation is used on the first and last phrase to reinforce the concept of musical form.

2. Create an original ostinato for the instruments while the class sings the song. Put the pattern of the ostinato on the board.

Round

1. Sing the song as a round in two, three, or four parts, depending upon the maturity of your class.

2. Step the pattern of the song as a round. For more mature students, divide the class into two, three, or four groups. Sing the song as a round and step or walk the pattern and turn the phrase. This activity can be done in circles.

EVALUATION OF RHYTHMIC AND PERCEPTUAL SKILLS

Psychomotor Development and Perception

1. Can the students maintain a rhythmic ostinato on instruments?
2. Can the students maintain a melodic ostinato or sing a round in two, three, or four parts?

Aural Acuity and Perception

1. Can the students recognize similarities and differences in phrases and melodic contour?
2. Can the students distinguish loud and soft? Phrasing? Low and high?

Visual Acuity and Perception

1. Can the students visualize a melody by gross or fine motor activities? Can they draw a picture of the melodic contour?
2. Can the students sing the song from the chart and use the repeat marks without losing the beat?

Echo

PREPARATION FOR THE CHART

Note: The three preceding charts presented the differences between beat *and* pattern, *the beat being steady and the pattern having long and short sounds and silence. Charts 14 and 15 develop this concept further through visual and motor perception (reading and writing the pattern). The "Evaluation of Rhythmic and Perceptual Skills" will follow Chart 15.*

INTRODUCE THE CHART

1. Tell the class to feel the beat inside of them before you start the chart. Start this beat by moving your hand up and down and saying "one, two, ready, begin." When you clap the first line of the chart, the class will echo you without losing the beat.

Teacher claps   Class echoes

Continue through the entire chart, keeping the beat and getting the complete feeling of the rest.

2. Choose one student to be the leader and clap the chart while the class echoes.
3. Clap the chart and give each pattern a different tone quality, which the class must echo:

   clap softly (*p*)
   rap knuckles on desk (*mf*)
   clap loudly (*f*)
   fingertips on desk (*p*)

4. Clap the chart and call on individual students to be the echo.
5. Clap the chart; class echoes and then speaks the rhythm syllables:

Teacher claps   Class claps

Class speaks

ta   ta   ta   rest
ti-ti ti-ti ta   rest
ta   ti-ti ta   ta
ta   ta   ta   rest

OTHER SONGS TO USE

- "Polly Wolly Doodle"

- "The Cuckoo"

- "Billy Boy"

Note: Many songs in the intermediate grades use rhythm patterns and note values that have not been introduced at this time. It may be necessary for you to review some of the folk songs of the lower grades that use rhythm patterns within the capabilities of the class.

ADDITIONAL ACTIVITIES

Dictation

Pass out paper and fold into fourths. On the chalkboard, draw a square divided into four sections, each section being numbered

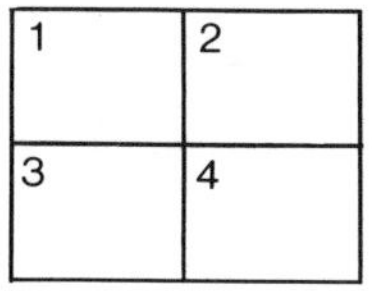

	Teacher claps	Class echoes
1.	I I I I	I I I I
2.	I ⊓ I I	I ⊓ I I
3.	I I I 𝄽	I I I 𝄽
4.	I 𝄽 ⊓ I	I 𝄽 ⊓ I

Class speaks	Class writes
ta ta ta ta	I I I I
ta ti-ti ta ta	I ⊓ I I
ta ta ta rest	I I I 𝄽
ta rest ti-ti ta	I 𝄽 ⊓ I

Choose individual students to fill in the squares on the chalkboard. How many students in the class wrote the pattern correctly? This activity should be done many times throughout the year.

Extended Patterns

1. Ask individuals in the class to clap a four beat pattern (for example, I I ⊓ I). The class will echo clap and say the rhythm syllables. The leader will then write the pattern on the chalkboard and draw a **bar line** (|). Choose another student to clap a pattern for the class to echo. Have the student write the chosen pattern next to the first one and draw another bar line. Explain that the bar lines separate the measures.

   I I ⊓ I | ⊓ ⊓ I I |

   Continue this activity for four measures, each pattern being different.

   I I ⊓ I | ⊓ ⊓ I I |
   I 𝄽 ⊓ I | I I 𝄽 I ‖

   Note: At this time, introduce the ***double bar,*** *which denotes the end of the pattern (or song). This is like a period at the end of a sentence (‖).*
2. Clap the entire four measures. These four measure patterns can be put on a chart for future use.
3. As the class becomes more confident, encourage them to make longer phrases or to make rhythm patterns of mystery songs that can be put on a chart and presented to the class. Be sure to make corrections if necessary, before presenting the charts to the class. The original charts can be song fragments or an entire song. Some of the students may wish to illustrate their charts.
4. Proceed to the next chart.

Left Hand-
Right Hand

Left Hand-Right Hand

Note: This chart introduces a different kind of two-part performance. The preceding charts have used two groups, two instruments, or clapping a pattern and walking or stepping the beat. Now, the two parts will be performed by the student, using their hands to execute both parts.

PREPARATION FOR THE CHART

1. The class will be seated at their desks and the fingertips of the right hand will tap the pattern and the knuckles of the left hand will rap the beat. This will provide differences in tone quality for each part performed.

   Note: The eraser end of a pencil, Popsicle sticks, coffee stirrers, or one chopstick will create an interesting tonal difference when played with one hand.

2. Sing a familiar song. Keep the beat with the left hand and tap the pattern with the right hand while singing; for example, "She'll Be Comin' 'Round the Mountain"

   Left hand: I |I I I I |I I I
   Right hand: ⊓|⊓ ⊓ ⊓ ⊓|I ⅔ ⅔

3. Repeat the above activity but do not sing (inner hearing). Establish the beat by saying, "One, two, ready, begin."

INTRODUCE THE CHART

1. Divide the class (left side, right side). Group 1 will read and clap the left hand pattern, and Group 2 will read and clap the right hand pattern of the first two lines of the chart using rhythm syllables.

2. Using the left hand knuckles and the right hand fingertips, read the two lines at the top of the chart, moving from left to right without losing the beat. This activity should be repeated slowly several times.

3. Select individual students to read the top two lines of the chart.

4. Select one student to read and clap the two lines at the bottom of the chart with rhythm syllables. Did the student observe the repeat signs (‖: :‖)?

5. Have the class read the bottom two lines of the chart with left and right hands, making the two sounds differ and observing the repeat bars.

6. *Canon:* it has been said that "All rounds are canons but not all canons are rounds." A **canon** is a rhythmic or tonal passage performed in two or more parts, each beginning at a different time.

Note: Canon clapping is a highly integrated activity and requires the aural and visual concentration needed to encourage students to read a written score. A rhythm canon can be written on the chalkboard and clapped or played on classroom instruments, much like singing a round.

To introduce the canon, (1) read and clap the entire pattern; (2) teacher begins clapping the pattern; (3) class begins clapping the pattern after the teacher has completed the first measure. Here is an example:

Teacher:
| | ⊓ | | ⊓⊓ | | | | ⧊ ⊓ | | | | ⧊ :‖

Class:
| | ⊓ | | ⊓⊓ | | | ⧊⊓ | | | | ⧊ :‖

Divide the class into two groups. Group 1 begins clapping; as soon as they have clapped one measure, Group 2 begins (do not expect complete success at first with canon clapping).

ADDITIONAL ACTIVITIES

1. Write the exercises below on the chalkboard. They are simple in order for the class to experience success and be able to progress to more difficult rhythm patterns.

Set 1:
Right hand: ⊓ | ⊓ ⊓   ⊓ | | | ‖
Left hand: ⊓ | ⊓ ⊓   ⊓ ⊓ | | ‖

Set 2:
Right hand: | | ⊓ | ⊓ ⊓ ⊓ | | | | ⧊ ‖
Left hand: ⊓ ⊓ | ⧊   ⊓ ⊓ ⊓ | | | | ⧊ ‖

2. Write a rhythm canon on the chalkboard that can be read and clapped by two groups, two individuals, or with two hands, depending on the maturity of the class.

1. | | | | | 2. ⧊⧊⧊⧊ | | | ⊓ | ⧊⧊⧊⧊ | | | | ⧊ ‖

3. Write the rhythm pattern of a familiar round on the board and read and clap or play on instruments.

"Are You Sleeping?"
‖: | | | | :‖: | | | ⧊ :‖: ⊓ ⊓ | | :‖: | | | ⧊ :‖

4. A truly exciting experience in aural perception is to clap a canon but *do not* put the pattern on the chalkboard. The class must listen to one pattern while clapping another. There are two approaches to this activity:

• Write a four measure pattern on the chalkboard. Tell the class that when you come to the end of the four measures you are going to continue clapping various rhythm patterns and the class must continue the canon.

• Begin with echo clapping for several measures. While clapping a pattern, say "canon" and proceed by not waiting for the echo.

EVALUATION OF RHYTHMIC AND PERCEPTUAL SKILLS

Psychomotor Development and Perception

1. Can the students hear a rhythm pattern and write the pattern on the chalkboard or paper?
2. Can they perform dual activities: left hand/ right hand, balance and laterality?

Aural Acuity and Perception

1. Can the students listen to one pattern and feel the beat while clapping or playing a different pattern (canon)?
2. Are they becoming increasingly aware of the silent beat (⧊)?

Visual Acuity and Perception

1. Are the students becoming increasingly confident and successful while reading rhythm patterns?
2. Can they recognize a song by its rhythm pattern?
3. Can the students read extended patterns with ease?

Low and High

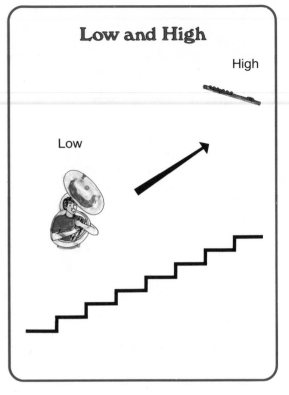

Low and High

High

Low

BELLS

Eleanor Kidd

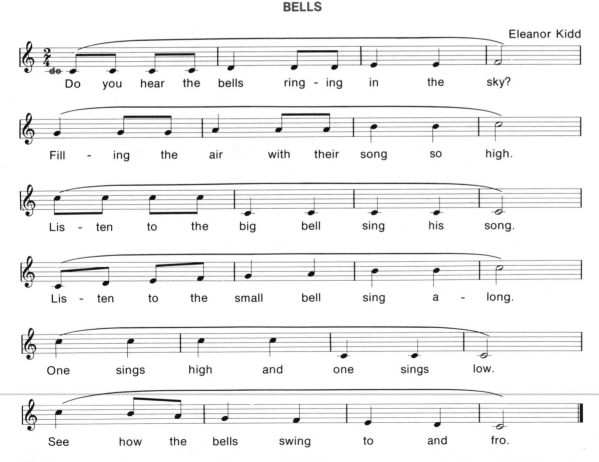

Do you hear the bells ring - ing in the sky?

Fill - ing the air with their song so high.

Lis - ten to the big bell sing his song.

Lis - ten to the small bell sing a - long.

One sings high and one sings low.

See how the bells swing to and fro.

Note: The concept of high and low pitch is a very abstract idea for students to conceive. To many students, "low" means soft and "high" means loud. This concept follows through to the upper grades, as any teacher of glee clubs and choruses knows so well.

PREPARATION FOR THE CHART

1. To develop the concept of *high* and *low* and *loud* and *soft,* use the language arts or story approach. One example of this is the sound of a siren on a fire engine heard in the distance, coming closer and closer, and then fading away. This exercise is invaluable to the individuals who have not yet learned to use their voices to create differences in pitch.

Note: It is not advisable to use the "down" and "up" terminology, because many instruments do not follow this rule. For example, on the piano, "down" is left and "up" is right; on the cello and double bass, "down" is high and "up" is low; and on the clarinet and saxophone, "down" is low.

2. Teach the song.
3. Sing the song and clap the pattern.

*Note: The **half note** (♩) will be introduced on a later chart. For this lesson, teach the half note by rote. The half note is held for two beats; clap the first beat and hold the second beat.*

4. Sing the song and use previous rhythm experiences; clap the beat • step or walk the beat • walk the beat and turn the phrase • clap or step the pattern.
5. Sing the song and dramatize the melodic contour with large arm movements. When the melody is "low," lower the arms and when the melody rises, or is "high," raise the arms.

INTRODUCE THE CHART

Note: Take out the resonator or song bells.

1. Point to the low bell on the chart. How low can the class make their voices (sound, not sing)? Imitate the low bell. *bong*
2. Point to the high bell. How high can the class make their voices? Imitate the high bell. *ting*
3. Imitate the sound of the bells and dramatize the low and high sounds with large arm movements.
4. Can the class make the low sound soft and then loud? (This is called *crescendo* and is symbolized as ◁══ .)

5. Can the class make the high sound loud and then soft? (This is called *decrescendo* and is symbolized as ══▷ .)
6. Sing or play a low note (for example, middle C) on the bells or piano. Sing a neutral syllable on this note and have the class match the tone with their voices ("ah" or "oh" with a relaxed jaw will give a good, full sound).
7. Sing or play the high note (C **octave**). Using a neutral syllable, sing the high note. Move from high to low several times and see if the class can match the tone.
8. Play a rhythm pattern on the bells or piano, moving from low to high. Have the class echo the pattern:

low	high	low,	low	high

high	low,	low	high	low

This activity can also be done with the teacher singing the low and high for the class to echo and using large arm movements.

9. Point to the stairs on the chart. Tell the class that melodies (songs) sometimes move in a stepwise fashion.

*Note: You may wish to play the C **scale** on the bells or piano to establish the stepwise concept.*

10. Point to the stairs on the chart and sing low C to high C, stepwise, on a neutral syllable (*loo*).
11. Sing "Bells" or any other song using a stepwise melody within an octave range. Point to the stairs on the chart while singing the song, moving from low to high with the melody.
12. Choose a leader to point to the chart while the class sings the song.

OTHER SONGS TO USE

"Lullaby Round" • "For Health and Strength" • "Do, Re, Mi"

ADDITIONAL ACTIVITIES

1. Sing the song "Bells" or any other song with a stepwise melody and make a picture in the air of the melodic contour. Use large arm movements and later make a picture of the melody on paper or the chalkboard.

Note: There will be many variations of this concept. Accept those that show an awareness of the melodic line.

2. Play the melody on the bells or piano as an accompaniment to the song.
3. If you have resonator bells, pass out the bells from middle C to the C above. Can the students discover and play the melody? Encourage the class to discover the melody, using their sense of rhythm and pitch to guide them.

EVALUATION OF RHYTHMIC AND PERCEPTUAL SKILLS

Psychomotor Development and Perception

1. Can the class dramatize the melodic contour of a song?
2. Can they draw the melodic contour in the air or on the chalkboard?

Aural Acuity and Perception

1. Can the students identify higher and lower pitches?
2. Can they identify and differentiate ascending and descending melodies?
3. Can they differentiate and produce vocally louder and softer tones (crescendo and decrescendo)?

Sol–Mi

Sol

Note: Although this is the first exposure to the sol–mi on a chart, it is hoped that you have used the roll call on sol–mi with the class since the beginning of the school year. Naturally, this would be taught by rote. The numbers on the chart (5 and 3) represent the numerical steps of the diatonic scale.

To the teacher with little musical training, there are several ways to find a minor third. On the piano or bells, from the lowest of three black notes to the black note below it or from G down to E are minor thirds.

Another way to find a minor third is to count three half-steps down. The only natural half-steps are between E and F, and B and C. The other half-steps are between white and black notes.

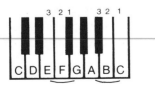

Mi

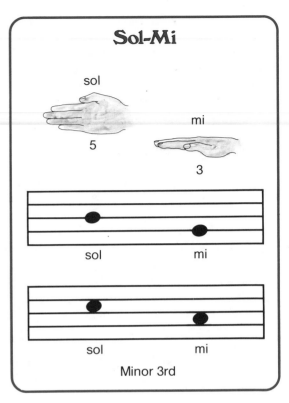

Sol-Mi

sol
5

mi
3

sol   mi

sol   mi

Minor 3rd

Sol *can begin on any note of the scale and* mi *is always three half-steps lower (minor third). This is important for the student who cannot match your* sol–mi *but sings a minor third either lower or higher. Match your* sol–mi *to the student's pitch so she or he will not feel embarassment.* Sol–mi *will be notated as s–m after being introduced.*

The sol–mi **interval** (minor third) *is the natural chant of children around the world. Children hailing their friends or calling their pets will often use the minor third or* sol–mi.

PREPARATION FOR THE CHART

1. Ask someone in the class to pretend he or she is calling a friend who is far down the street. "John–ny" is usually called by chanting sol–mi. Ask several students to demon-

strate how they would call their friend until someone calls on the minor third (*sol–mi*).

2. Ask one of the students to coax a little kitten to come to them. "Here, kitty, kitty, kitty" will usually be *sol, mi–mi, mi–mi, mi–mi.* Will the tone of voice be the same when calling the kitten as when calling "John–ny" (softer or louder)?

3. Teach the hand signal for *sol,* which is made by extending the hand, palm to the side, at chest level (see photograph).

4. Teach the hand signal for *mi,* which is made by extending the hand, palm down, at waist level (see photograph).

5. Walk from one student to another and sing his or her name with *sol–mi,* using hand signals. Each student will echo you by singing his or her name and using hand signals. Adapt the rhythm pattern to the syllables of the student's name.

6. Go around the room and sing each student's name with hand signals. The class will echo you, singing the student's name, using hand signals; then the student will sing his or her name with *sol–mi* and hand signals.

Note: This activity is especially effective for the student who needs peer recognition. Move quickly from one individual to another to avoid embarrassment for the insecure student. Be sure to insist on hand signals for sol–mi.

7. Call the roll by singing each student's name on *sol–mi.* The student answers "I'm here" or "pre–sent" on *sol–mi* with hand signals. If someone is absent, encourage the class to sing

⊓ | ⊓ |
"He's not here"   or   "She's not here"

on *sol–mi.* Try to keep the beat while doing this activity.

INTRODUCE THE CHART

Note: Hand singing is an integral part of the Threshold to Music *program. The use of hand singing in the intermediate grades plays an important role in the ability to hear and recognize intervals. Although arm signals were used in* Early Childhood *and* Level 1, *it has been found that the increased muscular coordination of the older student makes the use of hand singing more successful. These signals are illustrated on the charts. Hand signals for other tones of the* **diatonic** *scale will be introduced on later charts, and their consistent use will provide the students with an understanding of the intervals used to create a scale.*

1. Hold your hand over the hand signal for *sol* on the chart. Sing *sol.* The class will echo you and make the hand signal for *sol.*

2. Hold your hand over the hand signal for *mi* on the chart. Sing *mi.* The class will echo you and make the hand signal.

3. Using hand signals, place your hand directly under the note *sol* on the first musical **staff** of the chart and sing *sol.* Move slowly to the *mi* on the staff and sing *mi.* The class will echo you with hand signals.

4. Sing a slightly higher tone and repeat the above activity on the second musical staff of the chart.

Note: The notes on the chart are not absolute because there is not a **clef** *or* **key signature.** *The notes are presented to give the class the concept of* sol *being located on any line or space of the musical staff. This concept will be developed further on the following chart.*

OTHER SONGS TO USE

Tap out the pattern of familiar songs using *sol–mi* on the chart with hand signals

- "This Old Man"

  ⊓ | ⊓ |
  s m s s m s

- "Going Down to Cairo"

  ⊓ | ⊓ | |
  s s s s m s

- "Rain, Rain, Go Away"

  | | ⊓ |
  s m s s m

ADDITIONAL ACTIVITIES

1. Make flash cards of various rhythm patterns using *sol–mi:*

   | ⊓ | | ⊓ | ⊓ | | | ⊓ |
   s m m s m   s m s s m s   s s m m s

   Establish the pitch for *sol.* Hold up a flash card and have the class sing the pattern, using hand signals.

2. Use the flash cards with individual students, letting them establish their own pitch for *sol.*

3. Ask questions using *sol–mi* and hand signals, and let individual students answer with *sol–mi* and hand signals:

   Teacher: "Ma–ry, where's your book?"
   | | ⊓ | |
   s   m s   s   m

   Mary: "In the clo–set."
   | | | |
   s m s   m

4. Establish the pitch for *sol.* Using your hand over the hand signals or notes on one of the musical staves on the chart, indicate various rhythm patterns using *sol–mi,* but *do not* sing. Can the students sing the patterns you have indicated? Ask one student to be the leader. Let the student establish the pitch for *sol* and indicate the patterns on the chart.

5. Write the diatonic scale with tone syllables on the board or on a chart for future use. Number the syllables from one to eight:

do re mi fa sol la ti do^{l}
1   2   3   4   5   6   7   8

Point to *Sol*. What number is *sol* on the scale? *5* Point to *mi*. What number is *mi* on the scale? *3* This can also be done vertically to reinforce low and high and the position of various intervals on the scale.

do^{l}	8
ti	7
la	6
sol	5
fa	4
mi	3
re	2
do	1

6. Ask the class how many steps there are between *sol* and *mi* (count *sol* as 1). *3* Tell the class when they sing *sol–mi* they are singing a minor third.

Note: This concept will be developed further on future charts.

7. Point to the first musical staff on the chart. Tell the class that *sol* is "around" a line and *mi* is "around" the line below *sol*. It is recommended to use "around" the line rather than "on" the line, as in handwriting.

8. Point to the second musical staff on the chart. Tell the class that when *sol* is in a space, *mi* will be in the space below *sol*.

9. Sing *sol* while making the hand signal over the *sol* on the chart. Encourage the class to take a deep breath, open their mouths, and relax their jaws when they sing *sol*. This will produce a beautiful tone: As long as your hand is over the *sol*, the class will hold the tone, taking a breath whenever they feel the need. Do not push the tone by running out of air. This is called "supporting the tone." Try singing *sol* softly, then get louder, and then softer:

crescendo ⬿ decrescendo ⬾

Note: The pitch for sol *can start on any note of the scale, wherever it is comfortable for you and the class.*

10. Hold your hand over the *mi* on the chart, dropping your voice down to show the interval of a minor third. Sing *mi* with the hand sign. The class will echo with the hand sign. Tell the class to take a deep breath and smile without clenching the teeth when they sing *mi*. Hold the *mi* as long as your hand is over the *mi* on the chart. Sing *mi* with dynamics (⬿ ⬾).

11. Indicate various rhythm patterns on the chart, using hand signals for *sol–mi*. The class will sing the patterns with hand signals; for example:

❘ ❘ ⊓ ❘
s m·s s m

⊓ ❘ ⊓ ❘
s s m s s m

Note: Until the class is confident singing sol–mi, *begin these activities with the descending minor third (sol–mi), as the ascending minor third (mi–sol) is sometimes difficult for children to sing in tune.*

EVALUATION OF RHYTHMIC AND PERCEPTUAL SKILLS

Psychomotor Development and Perception

Can the class conceptualize the descending minor third with hand singing?

Aural Acuity and Perception

1. Can the majority of the class match the *sol–mi* with their voices?
2. Can the class recognize the minor third (*sol–mi*) in a familiar song?

Visual Acuity and Perception

Can the class recognize the descending minor third on the musical staff?

Here Is Sol–
Where Is Mi?

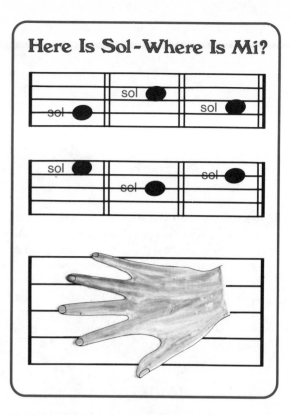

Note: This chart is used to develop the concept of movable do, *which is the basis of* **solmization** *(tone syllables) in the* Threshold to Music *series. This concept, introduced in the* Early Childhood *and* Level 1 *charts, should be presented after the class is confident with the interval of the minor third (sol–mi). It is not necessary to pitch the* sol *on any absolute note, such as G. Sol may be any pitch within the vocal or instrumental range. The hand represents the five lines of the musical staff.*

PREPARATION FOR THE CHART

1. Ask the class, "If *sol* is around a line, where is *mi*?" Mi *is around the line below sol. (Use the word* around *rather than on the line. This will eliminate confusion with writing words.)*
2. Ask the class, "If *sol* is in a space, where is *mi*?" Mi *is in the space below* sol.

INTRODUCE THE CHART

1. Point to the staff on the chart. How many lines does the class see? *five lines* How many spaces do they see? *four spaces* Number the lines, starting at the bottom, 1 through 5.
2. Point to each measure on the chart and ask individuals to find the *mi*. For example, ask, "If *sol* is around the second line, where is *mi*?" The student will answer "*Mi* is around the first line," and then come up to the chart to locate *mi* on the staff.

3. Point to the chart using hand signals, and sing the *sol* on varying pitches. Ask individual students to come up to the chart and point to the line or space for *mi* and sing the minor third below *sol,* using hand signals.
4. Choose individual students to be the leader and sing the *sol* and point to the chart. This student may choose someone to come up and sing the *mi* and find the note on the chart.

   Note: Be sure the pitch varies with the position of the note on the staff. Sol *on the second line will be lower in pitch than* sol *on the fourth space, even though the pitch is not absolute.*

5. Place your hand over the hand on the chart. Grasp one finger. This is to reinforce the

47

fact that the note goes "around" the line. Sing "Here is *sol*" on one note:

Then sing "Where is *mi*?" a minor third below:

Ask a student to show where *mi* is by grasping the finger below. When the student correctly identifies the position, he or she sings, "Here is *mi*," a minor third below *sol*.

6. Vary the finger and the pitch for *sol* and have the class sing the *mi*. Use the spaces by placing the *sol* between the fingers, remembering to raise and lower the pitch as shown on the chart.

ADDITIONAL ACTIVITIES

1. Move from student to student and hold out your hand with the fingers spread apart. Teacher sings "*sol* is here, where is *mi*?" on one pitch, grasping a finger:

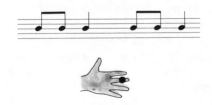

Student sings, "*mi* is here," grasping the finger below and singing the minor third.

Teacher sings, "*sol* is here, where is *mi*?" on a different pitch and uses a space:

Student sings the minor third, "*mi* is here," identifying the space:

2. Use mirror image and have the class identify *sol* and *mi* on their own hands as they sing the minor third. When the class is confident of the minor third, ask a student to be the leader.

EVALUATION OF RHYTHMIC AND PERCEPTUAL SKILLS

Aural and Visual Acuity and Perception

1. Can the students reproduce the repeated note with their voices?
2. Can they read the charts and reproduce the tones of the minor third?
3. Can they recognize and sing *sol* and *mi* on various pitches?

The Whole Rest

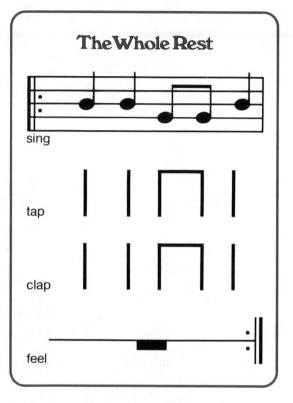

PREPARATION FOR THE CHART

To prepare the class for the chart use previous rhythmic and hand singing experiences:

- echo clapping
- inner hearing
- echo singing on *sol–mi,* using hand singing
- roll call

INTRODUCE THE CHART

1. Choose one student to read and clap the rhythm pattern of the first line while stepping the beat. Continue through the chart until you come to the last line.
2. Ask the class how many beats they feel for each line when they clap the pattern and step the beat. How many steps did they take for each line? *4*

3. Tell the class the last line is the symbol for the **whole rest** and to make the rest motion for each beat.

   Note: The class will remember the whole rest when you tell them that the whole rest gets the greatest number of beats and therefore, "hangs" from the line (━).

4. Establish the pitch for *sol,* and sing the first line with hand signals.
5. Continue through the chart with clapping, tapping, and feeling. Observe the repeat sign. Did the class retain the pitch (*sol*) while doing the other activities?
6. Select one student to read and sing the chart, using hand signals, without losing the beat. Did he or she retain the pitch for *sol*?

7. Repeat the chart several times, increasing the speed with each repetition.

   *Note: If your class is building a musical vocabulary, add the term **accelerando.** Compare it to a gas pedal on a car (accelerator). The class will immediately see the relationship.*

ADDITIONAL ACTIVITIES

1. Select one student to clap an original pattern and write it on the board; for example:

   ⊓ ⊓ | |

   Ask another student to place the syllables of his or her choice under the pattern, using the letters *s* and *m.* For example, a student might choose:

$$
\sqcap \ \ \sqcap \ \ | \ \ |
$$
s s m m s s

Sing the pattern, using hand signals.

2. Ask the class to compose their own rhythm pattern on *sol–mi.* Write them on large pieces of paper to present to the class.

3. Make flash cards for *clap, tap, feel, step,* and the *whole rest.*

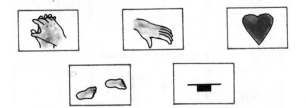

Write a four measure rhythm pattern with repeat bars on *sol–mi.* Ask the class to follow the directions on the flash cards without losing the beat. (Change the cards at the end of four beats.)

$$
\| : \ | \ \sqcap \ | \ \xi \ | \ \sqcap \ \ \sqcap \ | \ |
$$
s m m s   s s m m s

$$
| \ \xi \ \sqcap \ | \ \sqcap \ \xi \ \sqcap \ | \ : \|
$$
s   s s m   m m   s s s

4. Use this chart or flash cards to give the class a break in the regular school day. This is especially effective when used to refresh a tired class. Some other charts to use for this purpose are "Inner Hearing," "Rhythms," and "Scotland's Burning."

EVALUATION OF RHYTHMIC AND PERCEPTUAL SKILLS

Psychomotor Development and Perception

Can the class recognize and feel silence while keeping the beat (whole rest)?

Aural Acuity and Perception

Can the class retain a given pitch while engaging in diverse motor activities?

Toy Symphony

Toy Symphony

ta ti-ti ta ti-ti ta ti-ti   ti-ti ta ti-ti-di ti-ti

sol

sol

The ability to listen plays a very important role in the student's learning program. This is a skill that should be taught in much the same manner as reading and number concepts. Too often both student and teacher are besieged with background sounds, for example, music in the grocery store, dentist's office, and so on. As a result the listening part of our musical experience has often been misused, abused, or neglected completely.

Many people do not realize the wonderful ways in which symphonies, concertos, and even simple songs are constructed. It is exciting to listen for repetition of themes and rhythms, key changes, and instrumental entries. With the understanding of the architecture of music comes an ever greater appreciation and, thus, more enjoyment of it.

Not every classroom teacher or all the students in a class are going to be able to hear and understand all the complex parts of a composition, but it is possible to learn to hear and identify many new things.

Note: In order to use this chart you will need a recording of the "Toy Symphony." Contact the music department for assistance in finding the record.

PREPARATION FOR THE CHART

1. Tell the class the story of Joseph Haydn (pronounced *hīd–n*).

   Joseph Haydn was born in Austria in 1732, the same year George Washington was born. (Find Austria on a map or globe. Subtract 1732 from the present year. How long ago was Joseph Haydn born?) When Haydn was five years old, he was sent to a neighboring village to study music. When he was eight years old, he left for the large city of Vienna to sing in a church choir. Although many times he went hungry, he always kept his happy disposition. He studied hard and began to write music when he was seventeen years old.

   One day, a wealthy prince, Prince Esterhazy, hired him as a music master. The prince had a large castle with many rooms and everyone who worked for him lived in the castle. It was Haydn's duty to teach the musicians and keep them in practice so they would be ready to play for concerts, at mealtimes, and for dancing. In addition to composing all the music he also had to see that the musicians behaved politely, wore clean clothes, and powdered their wigs.

Haydn once went to a toy fair and was so delighted with the music-making toys he wanted to buy them, even though he had no children of his own. After all, his own musicians called him "Papa," so why shouldn't he compose a little symphony using toy instruments?

The only real instruments used in the "Toy Symphony" are violins and bass viols. Instead of woodwinds, he used bird whistles—the cuckoo and the trilling nightingale. For brasses, he used tin trumpets; and for percussion, a triangle, a rattle, and a tin drum.

2. Introduce pictures of the string family. Can the students identify the violin and bass viol (sometimes called the bass fiddle)? Which instrument will have a high voice? *violin* Is it large or small? *small* Which instrument will have a low voice? *bass viol* Is it large or small? *large*

3. If you have an instrumental program in your school, invite some of the students to demonstrate playing the string instruments and the trumpet.

4. Play the first movement of a recording of the "Toy Symphony."

   • Did the class recognize the cuckoo and the nightingale?

   • How did the tin trumpet sound? If anyone in the class plays the trumpet, ask him or her to demonstrate the part of the tin trumpet.

   • Ask the class to clap the pattern of the trumpet.

INTRODUCE THE CHART

1. Read and clap the rhythm pattern at the top of the chart. Does the class notice something new? ⊓⊓ *ti–ti-di* What instruments play this pattern on the recording of the "Toy Symphony?"

*Note: These (⊓ ti-di) are **sixteenth notes** and should be taught by rote for now. They will be developed further in Level 2. There are two sixteenth notes to each eighth note, so naturally they will be twice as fast.*

Be sure to observe the repeat signs without losing the beat. Play the first section of the recording and ask the class to identify the theme using rhythm syllables.

2. Clap the pattern of the cuckoo, and then sing the pattern using hand signals.

Note: When using hand signals, make the motion for the rest with one hand.

Continue playing the record and identify the cuckoo theme with hand signals.

3. Clap the pattern of the tin trumpet, using the rhythm syllables for the sixteenth notes (⊓⊓ I *ti–ti-di ta*). Now sing the pattern with hand signals. (Maintaining the same pitch can sometimes present a problem.) Play the record and identify the trumpet with hand signals.

4. Play the entire first movement and identify the parts on the chart.

ADDITIONAL ACTIVITIES

1. Play the record and let the class count how many times they hear the theme for the cuckoo.

2. Divide the class. Have one group make the hand signals for the cuckoo theme, and the other group clap the pattern of the tin trumpet, while listening to the record.

3. Another listening activity is to have the class sit absolutely silent for three minutes. Ask the class to make a list of the sounds they heard (a bird? an automobile horn? footsteps? a lawnmower? and so on).

EVALUATION OF RHYTHMIC AND PERCEPTUAL SKILLS

Psychomotor Development and Perception

1. Can the class relate the interval of the descending minor third (*sol–mi*) with hand signals?

2. Can the students clap the pattern of the sixteenth note?

Aural and Visual Acuity and Perception

1. Can the students listen and identify different themes?

2. Can the students read a pattern and identify the theme being played?

Question and Answer

Note: Charts 21, 22, and 23 reinforce the descending and ascending minor third (sol–mi, mi–sol). Draw the class's attention to the fact that if sol *is around a line,* mi *will be around the line below* sol. *If* sol *is in a space,* mi *will be in the space below* sol. *The "Evaluation of Rhythmic and Perceptual Skills" will appear at the end of Chart 23.*

PREPARATION FOR THE CHART

1. Echo sing several rhythm patterns using the descending and ascending minor third with hand signals. For example:

| | | |
s m m s

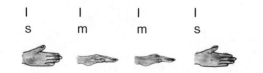

s   s   s   s

l
m   m   m

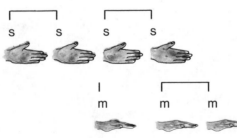

2. Echo sing several rhythm patterns using repeated notes.

Note: The repeated note may cause some difficulty at first because the natural tendency is to move to another note, usually down a minor third.

For example:

| ⌐⌐ ⌐⌐ |
s m m m m s

⌐⌐ ⌐⌐ | |
s s s s m s

3. Sing rhythmic questions on *sol–mi* with hand signals. Choose individual students to answer with hand signals.

Teacher:
"What shall we play to–day?"
| ⌐⌐ ⌐⌐ |
s m m s s m

Student:
"Let's play bas–ket–ball."
| · | ⌐⌐ |
s m s s m

4. Longer sentences can be used to reinforce the concept of repeated notes.

53

Teacher:

"Mar—y, will you pass out pen—cils

s   s s s   s   s s   s

to the ones who need them?"

m m m   m   s   s

Student:

"Ev—ery one who needs a pen—cil,

s s   s s   s   ss   s

raise your hand."

m   m   m

Note: There will be variations, but accept those patterns that use the minor third (sol—mi).

INTRODUCE THE CHART

1. Select one student to clap the pattern of the chart, disregarding the division of the measure. The class will echo if the pattern clapped is correct.
2. Sing the entire chart with tone syllables (*sol—mi*) and hand signals, keeping the beat as you move from line to line of the chart.
3. Teacher sings the left side of the chart with hand signals, and the class will sing the right side of the chart using hand signals.

Note: Unless the class is confident with the descending minor third, you may experience some difficulty with the ascending minor third (mi—sol).

4. Divide the class into two groups. Group 1 will sing the left side of the chart with hand signals, Group 2 will sing the answer with hand signals. The answer is not an echo. Later, ask individual students to sing the chart. One student sings the question and another sings the answer. Be sure the starting pitch for *sol* is established by the leader. The answer must use the pitch given by the leader. It is not important what starting tone is used for *sol,* but the interval of the minor third must be correct relative to the pitch of *sol.* Remember, as a teacher you are to listen more often than you sing.
5. Divide the class. Ask Group 1 to sing and sustain *sol* while Group 2 sings the entire chart with tone syllables and hand signals (ostinato). Take a breath at the beginning of each line of the chart in order to provide proper breath support, keep the pitch, and prevent the tone from becoming forced. Repeat the above activity while Group 1 sings the chart and Group 2 sings *mi.*

ADDITIONAL ACTIVITIES

1. Create a conversation to fit the pattern on the chart, using questions and answers; for example:

Hel—lo   Hel—lo

s m   m s

How are you?   I am fine.

s s m   m m s

Continue through the entire chart.

2. Encourage the students to write original "conversations" or original poems. Write the rhythm symbols and tone syllables under the words using *s—m.* These can be put on the chalkboard or large pieces of paper to use as classroom charts.

Conversation:

Can I play first base?

s s m s m

You be the catch—er.

s m m s   m

Poetry:

Hap—py, hair—y, drool—ing dog.

s s m ms   s m

He's my dog with fleas.

s s s   m

3. Proceed to the next chart.

Sing Together

Note: This lesson will incorporate the skills of reading, singing, and writing music.

PREPARATION FOR THE CHART

1. Review echo singing, using student leaders. For the more musically proficient class, begin some of the patterns on *mi.* For example:

Leader	Class
⌐ ⌐	⌐ ⌐
m s m m s	m s m m s
⌐ ⌐ ⌐	⌐ ⌐ ⌐
m m s s m	m m s s m

Note: Be sure to insist on the use of hand signals and to take careful note of the spatial relationship of the intervals.

INTRODUCE THE CHART

1. Select a student to clap the pattern of the first line of the chart. If the pattern is correct, the class will echo; if the pattern is incorrect, the class will remain silent.
2. Select another student to clap the pattern of the second line of the chart, repeating the above activity.
3. Give the class an opportunity to decide how the third line should be performed.

*Note: When two parts are performed simultaneously, the stems of the notes are often reversed, particularly in vocal music. When two groups perform simultaneously, they are known as an **ensemble.** When two individuals perform simultaneously, they are known as a **duet** (see list of Musical Terms).*

4. Select one student to read and clap the top notes of Line 3, then select another student to read and clap the bottom notes of Line 3. Ask the two students to perform both parts simultaneously. (You will probably have to establish the beat.)
5. Establish the pitch for *sol.*

Note: This can be given by the teacher singing or using the piano, bells, or recorder.

Ask one student to sing the first line of the chart with hand signals. If the melodic pattern is sung correctly, the class will echo, and if the melodic pattern is incorrect, they will remain silent.

6. Choose another student to sing the second line of the chart, repeating the above activity.
7. Ask the class to sing the top notes of Line 3 and then sing the bottom notes.

55

8. Divide the class. Group 1 sings the first line, Group 2 sings the second line. Both groups sing the third line simultaneously (ensemble).

Note: This last activity may take some repitition before being completely successful. Do not spend time in drilling or the class will lose interest.

9. Select two students to perform the entire chart. Provide many opportunities for students to perform this chart individually (duet).

ADDITIONAL ACTIVITIES

1. Establish the pitch for *sol*. Teacher makes the hand signals but *does not* sing. Class sings the pattern with hand signals.

Teacher

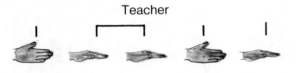

Class sings

| | ⊓ | |

s m m s m

2. Use individual staff charts on heavy paper and cut out notes of black paper. Distribute the staff and notes to the class. Designate on which line or space *sol* will be.

Teacher sings with hand signals

| | ⊓ |

s m s s m

Class echoes and places notes

Use many variations of rhythm patterns containing *sol–mi.* You can also put the staff on the chalkboard and let individual students write the pattern after it is sung.

3. *Variation of the above activity:* Establish the pitch and position of *sol* on the staff.

Hand signals without singing

Class sings and places the notes

4. Play various patterns on the recorder, bells, or piano. Establish the position of *sol* on the staff.

Play

| ⊓ | |

G E E G E

Class sings with hand signals and places the notes

| ⊓ | |

s m m s m

5. Proceed to the next chart.

What Do You Hear?

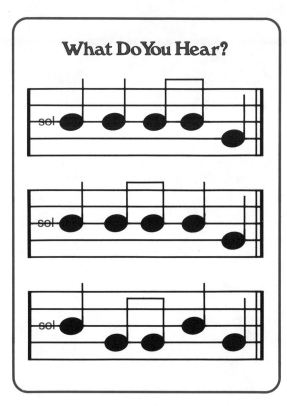

PREPARATION FOR THE CHART

This chart is used for testing the class on the concept of *sol–mi*. This will be the first time they will sing and read the minor third using various rhythm patterns.

INTRODUCE THE CHART

1. Clap each rhythm pattern with rhythm syllables.
2. Choose individual students to clap a line of their choice on the chart. The class will identify the pattern by holding up the correct number of fingers.
3. Ask one student to sing the pattern of her or his choice. The class will identify the pattern. *1, 2, or 3*

- *Variation:* If the melodic pattern is sung correctly, the class will echo the leader. If sung incorrectly, the class will remain silent.
4. Sing one of the patterns on "loo" and have the class echo with tone syllables and hand singing.
5. Use hand signals for one of the patterns without singing. The class will sing the pattern with hand signals. Ask for volunteers to identify each pattern sung.

EVALUATION OF RHYTHMIC AND PERCEPTUAL SKILLS

Psychomotor Development and Perception

1. Can the students write melodic patterns containing *sol–mi* on the musical staff?

2. Are they developing the spatial relationship of the interval of the minor third (*sol–mi*)?

Aural Acuity and Perception

1. Are the students becoming increasingly confident while singing the minor third?
2. Can they hear the minor third and write the interval on the musical staff?
3. Can they perform musical patterns on *sol–mi* in two parts?

Visual Acuity and Perception

1. Can the students identify the minor third in varying positions on the musical staff?
2. Can they read a melodic pattern with increasing confidence?

A New Note–La

La

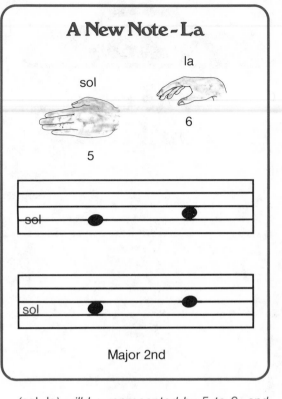

A New Note–La

sol   la

5   6

sol

sol

Major 2nd

Note: Charts 24 and 25 introduce the note la. *The "Evaluation of Rhythmic and Perceptual Skills" for these charts appears after Chart 25.*

PREPARATION FOR THE CHART

The intervals of the major second (*sol–la*) and the perfect fourth (*mi–la*) are found in many playground chants, singing games, and American folk songs. For example:

- "It's raining, it's pouring . . ."
- "Johnny has a sweetheart"
- "I'm bigger than you are"

INTRODUCE THE CHART

1. Tell the class they are going to learn a new note that is called *la*. Demonstrate the *la* with hand signals while singing the note.

The interval can be played on the bells, piano, or recorder (*G* to *A*).

Note: Pull the la *up from the* sol *position and tell the class that* la *wants to go back to* sol. *This is the nature of the interval, and also keeps the two notes in relationship to the distance of the notes on the staff.*

2. Sing *sol–la* with hand signals. The class will echo with hand signals. Sing various patterns using *sol–la*.
3. Ask the class to explain the numerals *5* and *6* on the chart. (If necessary, review the vertical scale in Lesson 17.)

Note: The descending minor third (sol–mi) will be represented by the numerals 5 to 3 on the numerical scale. The major second

(*sol–la*) *will be represented by 5 to 6, and the perfect fourth (la–mi), by 6 to 3. This is a simplified explanation, but it will prove invaluable to the student with musical talent, even though it is a rote experience.*

4. Tap out various rhythm patterns on the chart with hand signals.

    ❘ ⊓ ❘ ❘   ❘ ❘ ⊓ ❘
    s ❘ ❘ s ❘   ❘ s ❘ ❘ s

5. Choose one student to lead the class in the above activity.
6. Tell the class that if *sol* is around a line, the *la* will be in the space directly above. The same will apply to the *sol* in a space. The *la* would be around the line above. Demonstrate this on the chart with hand signals.

ADDITIONAL ACTIVITIES

1. Many students will understand the concept of intervals by using the vertical scale shown in Lesson 17.

   Note: The difference between the major third and the minor third can be demonstrated visually by the use of a piano keyboard or a full set of resonator bells. The minor third has three half steps (Lesson 17), while the major third has four half steps.

   Major and minor thirds:

   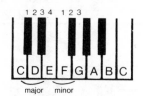

The major second has two half steps while the minor second has one half step.

Major and minor seconds:

The perfect intervals have a very complicated definition, which goes into the physics of sound. If you are fortunate enough to have some students who wish to do some research in this area, refer them to the Harvard Dictionary of Music *and* Grove's Dictionary of Music and Musicians. *The class might be interested in the fact that when a perfect interval becomes inverted, it remains perfect; for example, a perfect fourth, when inverted, becomes a perfect fifth (la up to mi). Other intervals when inverted change from major to minor or minor to major; for example, a minor third when inverted becomes a major sixth, and a major second when inverted becomes a minor seventh. This is an overly simplified explanation of major, minor, and perfect intervals. The concept of intervals should be developed aurally at this level.*

2. Ask several students to discover various intervals on a keyboard by counting the half steps.

3. Proceed to the next chart.

Where Is La?

Where Is La?

INTRODUCE THE CHART

1. Sing the first line of the chart with hand signals with the class. Ask several students to sing the first line for the class to echo.
2. Before you introduce the second line of the chart, ask the class if they have ever said, "I'm bigger than you are" to someone on the playground. Ask several students to demonstrate how they would say it.
3. When one student has chanted

   "I'm big—ger than you are"

   have the class echo and clap the rhythm pattern.

4. Sing the chant, clap the rhythm pattern, and step the beat. How many times did they clap for the second beat? Let the class discover that there were three claps to one beat.

   Note: This will be an introduction to the **triplet** (), *which will be used on succeeding charts. The rhythm syllables for the triplet are "tri—ple—ti."*

5. Clap the pattern of Line 2 on the chart with rhythm syllables:

   ta tri-ple-ti ta ta

6. Ask one student to sing Line 2 of the chart with tone syllables and hand signals.

7. Place your hand over the hand on the chart. Grasp one finger and sing on one note:

   "*Sol* is here, where is *la*?"

   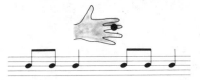

   Ask one student to come up and show where *la* is and sing:

   "*La* is here."

8. Change the pitch and position of *sol* to a space and repeat the above activity.

9. Using these same activities, include the syllable *mi* (perfect fourth).

OTHER SONGS TO USE

- "A–tisket, A–tasket"

  ♪ | | ⊓ | | ⊓ | ⊓ ⊓ | | |
  s   s s m l   s m m s s m l   s m

- "Tideo"

  | | | | | | | | ≀
  m s s l   m s s

- "French Cathedrals"

  | | | ≀ | | | | ≀
  s l m   s l m

ADDITIONAL ACTIVITIES

1. Use echo clapping with the triplet:

Teacher claps	Class echoes and then says
		⌢3⊓		ta ta tri-ple-ti ta
⌢3⊓	⌢3⊓		tri-ple-ti ta tri-ple-ti ta
	≀ ⌢3⊓		ta rest tri-ple-ti ta

2. Make flash cards of rhythm patterns using the triplet. Move around the room so that each student will have an opportunity to clap a pattern. This can be an exciting activity if you can move from student to student without losing the beat.

3. Use echo clapping and mirror image with the triplet pattern:

   Tapping | ≀ ⌢3⊓ |

   Stepping | ⌢3⊓ | |

   Slapping knees ⌢3⊓ ⌢3⊓ | |

4. Establish the pitch for *sol.* Make hand signals of various patterns using *sol–la–mi* without singing. Class echoes, singing the pattern with hand signals:

Teacher

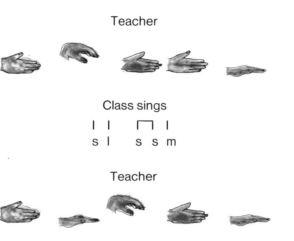

Class sings

| | | ⊓ | |
s l   s s m

Teacher

Class sings

| ⊓ | |
s m l s   m

5. Make flash cards of various patterns using *sol–la–mi.* Let the class or individuals sing the pattern, using hand signals.

| | ⌢3⊓ |
s l s s s m

| | ⊓ | |
l s l l m

⌢3⊓ ⌢3⊓ | |
s s s l l l s m

6. For the class that understands the concept of the interval, sing various intervals with syllables beginning with the minor third (*sol–mi*), and have the students echo with interval names and hand signals.

Teacher

⊓ | ⊓ |
s s m   s s m

⊓ ⊓ ⊓ ⊓
s s l l s s l l

⊓ | ⊓ |
| | m | | m

Class sings

| ⊓ | | ⊓ | |
mi - nor   third   mi - nor   third
s   s   m   s   s   m

⊓ ⊓ ⊓ ⊓
ma - jor   sec-ond ma - jor   sec-ond
s   s   l   l   s   s   l   l

⊓ | ⊓ |
per-fect fourth   per-fect fourth
l   l   m   l   l   m

7. *Title Game:* Find the name of states that have a triplet pattern and create a descriptive phrase. Write the pattern:

Oregon rain	⌢3⊓	
Wisconsin cheese	⌢3⊓	
Washington apples	⌢3⊓ ⊓

8 Use a pattern with triplets as an ostinato to a familiar song, either clapping, tapping, or using instruments. For example, with "Are You Sleeping?" use:

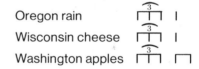

Note: These activities require an ever-increasing amount of perception and concentration on the part of the student. Many of the activities will need repetition, though not necessarily on the same day or lesson. The more complex and integrated the activities, the more they should be performed with various familiar songs, combining previous rhythmic and melodic experiences.

EVALUATION OF RHYTHMIC
AND PERCEPTUAL SKILLS

Psychomotor Development and Perception

1. Can the students maintain a rhythmic ostinato using triplets while singing a song?
2. Can the students perform hand signals with increasing confidence and with the proper spatial relationship for each interval?

Aural Acuity and Perception

2. Can the students hear and sing the interval of the major second and of the perfect fourth?
2. Can they clap the triplet pattern and keep the beat?

Visual Acuity and Perception

1. Can the students recognize the intervals of the major second (*sol–la*) and perfect fourth (*la–mi*) on the staff?
2. Can they write the intervals on the staff, using the correct lines or spaces for *sol, la,* and *mi*?

Camptown Races

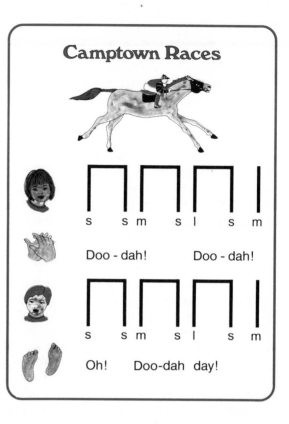

Camptown Races

s   s m   s l   s   m

Doo - dah!   Doo - dah!

s   s m   s l   s   m

Oh!   Doo-dah day!

CAMPTOWN RACES

Stephen Foster

sol
Camp-town la - dies sing this song,

Doo - dah!   Doo - dah!

Camp-town race - track five miles long,

Oh,   Doo - dah - day!

Chorus

sol
Goin' to run all night,

Goin' to run all day!   I'll

bet my mon-ey on a bob - tail nag,

Some bod - y bet on the bay.

Note: Charts 26, 27, and 28 teach and reinforce the same basic learning experience. Therefore, the "Evaluation of Rhythmic and Perceptual Skills" is presented at the end of Chart 28.

PREPARATION FOR THE CHART

Note: There are many verses to this famous song, which can be found in folk song books.

1. Teach the song.
2. Sing the song and use previous rhythm experiences:

   - clap the pattern and step the beat
   - step the pattern, walk the beat, and turn the phrase
   - clap as a mystery song

- practice inner hearing
- sing the song and clap or step an ostinato

3. You may wish to introduce your class to the music of Stephen Foster through recordings.

INTRODUCE THE CHART

1. Ask one student to clap the rhythm pattern on the chart with rhythm syllables.
2. Ask another student to sing the tone syllables of the first line with hand signals. The class will clap and sing the next line ("Doo—dah").
3. Ask for a volunteer to sing the next line with hand signals; everyone sings and steps the last line.
4. Sing the entire chart with hand signals, but put the "Doo—dah's" (second and fourth lines) inside (inner hearing).
5. Sing the first and third line of the chart with hand signals and follow the directions on the chart for "Doo—dah!" (clap and step).
6. Choose one student to sing the syllables with hand signals; have the class sing the "Doo—dah's," being careful not to lose the beat. The entire class sings the chorus while stepping the beat. A variation of this activity is to perform a different activity for each phrase. This can be done with the inner hearing flash cards; for example,

- step the pattern for the first phrase
- clap the pattern for the second phrase
- use inner hearing for the third phrase
- sing the last phrase

7. Sing the song with words and hand signals.
8. If the class has learned other verses to the song, let individual students sing the first and third phrases with words and hand signals; the class sings the "Doo—dah's." All join in on the chorus.

OTHER SONGS TO USE

Put some fragments using *sol—la—mi* on the chalkboard or on a large chart for future use. Sing the words or use rhythm activities for those portions of the song where the tone syllables are unfamiliar:

- "Up on the Housetop"

  s s l s m   clap   l l s m   clap

- "Rain, Rain, Go Away"

  s m s s m s s m l s s m

- "Tideo"

  m s s l   m s s

ADDITIONAL ACTIVITIES

1. Sing the song, making large arm movements for each phrase:

   Camptown ladies sing this song,

   Doo-dah, Doo-dah!

   Continue through the entire song.

2. On a large piece of paper or on the chalkboard, draw a picture of the melody line. For example:

   Phrase 1:   Phrase 2:

   Continue through the entire song.

3. Have the class decide which phrases are the same and which are different. Use geometric shapes or letters. For example:

   - Phrase 1: ●
   - Phrase 2: ▲
   - Phrase 3: ●
   - Phrase 4: ■

   Encourage the class to discover similarities and differences of other familiar songs. This activity will be invaluable to them when they begin to study form in music.

4. Proceed to the next chart.

27 Mystery Songs

PREPARATION FOR THE CHART

As a general preparation, sing various patterns using *sol–la–mi* with hand signals and echo singing. Establish the pitch for sol:

Teacher   Class

s	l	l	s	m		s	l	l	s	m
l	l	s	l	l	s		l	l	s	l	l	s

Begin some of the patterns on *mi:*

m	s	l	s	m		m	s	l	s	m
m	l	s	m	m		m	l	s	m	m

Tideo

1. Teach the song.
2. Sing the song and use previous rhythmic experiences (refer to Lesson 11). Encourage free, relaxed movements.
3. Walk the beat and sing only the first word of each measure (accent):

Pass – – – | Ti – – –
Pass – – – | Ti – – –

and so on.

1. TIDEO

U.S. Singing Game

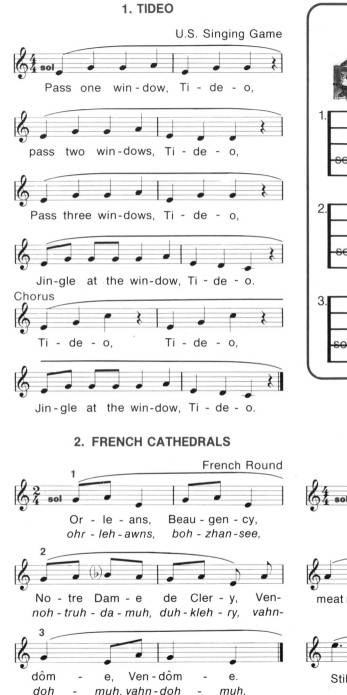

Pass one win-dow, Ti - de - o,

pass two win-dows, Ti - de - o,

Pass three win-dows, Ti - de - o,

Jin-gle at the win-dow, Ti - de - o.

Chorus

Ti - de - o, Ti - de - o,

Jin-gle at the win-dow, Ti - de - o.

2. FRENCH CATHEDRALS

French Round

1 Or - le - ans, Beau - gen - cy,
ohr - leh - awns, boh - zhan - see,

2 No - tre Dam - e de Cler - y, Ven -
noh - truh - da - muh, duh - kleh - ry, vahn -

3 dôm - e, Ven - dôm - e.
doh - muh, vahn - doh - muh.

3. HEY, HO! NOBODY HOME

English Round

Hey, ho! No - bod-y home. No

meat nor drink nor mon-ey have I none;

Still I will be ver - y mer - ry!

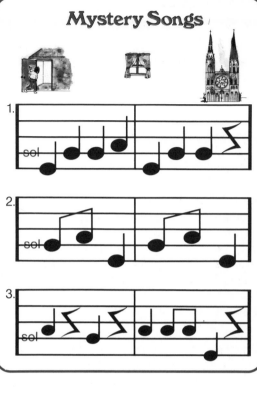

Mystery Songs

1. sol
2. sol
3. sol

French Cathedrals

1. Teach the song (be aware of the B flat (♭) in the third measure).
2. Sing the song and step the beat. How many beats do you feel? 2
3. Sing the song and sway back and forth to the beat.

Hey, Ho! Nobody Home

1. Teach the song.
2. Sing the song and use previous rhythmic experiences.

*Note: Teach the **dotted** quarter **note** and single eighth note by rote (♩ ♪) when clapping the pattern. These will be introduced on a later chart. The rhythm syllables are ta—a and ti, respectively.*

INTRODUCE THE CHART

1. Choose individual students to clap the rhythm pattern of each song. Many students in the class will be able to identify the songs by their rhythm patterns (mystery songs).
2. If a student identifies the song correctly, ask him or her to sing the phrase on the chart with hand signals.
3. Have a volunteer choose a phrase on the chart and do only the hand signals, without singing. Have the class identify the melody by holding up the number of fingers that correspond to the number of the line on the chart.

ADDITIONAL ACTIVITIES

Tideo

Note: The traditional singing game is more appropriate for the children of the primary grades. The chorus, however, can be done by students of the intermediate grades.

1. Sing the song while facing a partner. While singing the chorus, make the following motions with your partner:

Ti—	*slap own knees*
de—	*clap own hands*
o	*touch fists of partner*
Jingle	*slap knees*
at the	*clap own hands*
win—	*partners clap right hands*
dow	*clap own hands*
Ti—	*partners clap left hands*
de—	*clap own hands*
o	*fists on knees*

Note: The use of the fist is to prepare the class for the do syllable.

2. Sing the song and draw a picture of the melodic contour on a large piece of paper.

Phrase 1: Phrase 2:
Phrase 3: Phrase 4:
Phrase 5: Phrase 6:

Note: Each student's picture will be different. Accept those that show an understanding of melody line and form (similarities and differences). An interesting art project is to make the melodic phrases in different colors with heavy crayon and wash with water color.

French Cathedrals

1. After the song is learned, divide the class and sing as a two- or three-part round. When the first group comes to the end of the round, continue singing "Vendôme" on la—sol—mi until all groups come to the end of the song.
2. Divide the class. One group sings sol—mi or sol—la—mi with syllables or words ("ding— dong" or "ding, ding, dong") as an ostinato while the second group sings the song. Use hand signals for the ostinato.
3. Encourage the class to decide on the dynamics to be used. Where should the song be soft (*p*) and where should it get louder (crescendo ⟨)?

Hey, Ho! Nobody Home

1. After the song is learned, divide the class and sing as a round.
2. Create an instrumental ostinato, taking the pattern from the melody:

- Wood block:
  "Nobody home"
- Triangle or sticks:
  "Money have I none"

Ask the class to decide which instrument or sound fits the mood of the song. Have one group sing the song, or sing as a round, while several ostinatos are playing the accompaniment. Let the instruments set the beat before the singers begin.

3. Play the song as a three-part round without singing, using a different sound for each entry:

- Group 1: tap pattern on book
- Group 2: clap softly
- Group 3: pat knees

4. Divide the class and form two circles, one inside the other. Walk the beat (two steps to the measure) while singing the song as a two-part round. Change direction on each phrase. Group 2 stands still until beginning the song.
5. Proceed to the next chart.

What Do You Hear?

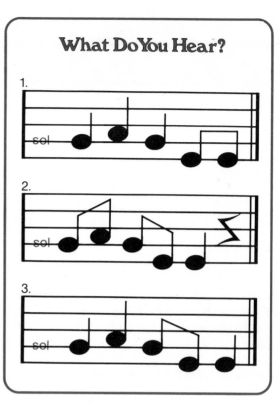

Note: This chart is used for testing the concept of sol–la (major second). The activity involves the reading of the rhythm pattern, the reading of notes on the staff, and the ability to read and sing the correct intervals. If the previous charts have been thoroughly understood, the class will experience the gratifying feeling of success at their ability to read music.

INTRODUCE THE CHART

1. Choose one student to clap the rhythm pattern of Line 1 of the chart. If clapped correctly, the class will echo. If clapped incorrectly, they will remain silent. Continue through the entire chart, choosing a different student for each line of the chart.

2. Review the syllable names on the chart. The class will discover that the melody is the same, only the rhythm pattern is different.

3. Sing one of the melodies on the chart, using tone syllables and hand signals. Tell the class to raise one finger if they heard Melody 1, two fingers if it was Melody 2, and so on. Ask for a volunteer to sing one of the melodies for the class to identify.

4. Choose any one of the melodies on the chart. Make the hand signals, but do not sing. Can the class identify the melody? Ask individual students to perform this activity.

5. Sing one of the melodies on a neutral syllable ("loo"). Let the class echo you with tone syllables and hand signals. Ask individual students to lead the class in this activity.

EVALUATION OF RHYTHMIC AND PERCEPTUAL SKILLS

Psychomotor Development and Perception

1. Can the students sing a song and maintain a rhythmic, vocal, or instrumental ostinato?
2. Can they move freely with increased coordination and body awareness?

Aural and Visual Acuity and Perception

1. Can the students sing a major second while reading the interval on the staff?
2. Can they recognize the major second (sol–la) on the musical staff?

Mi–La

Note: Lessons 29 and 30 introduce the interval of the perfect fourth (mi–la) on the staff. The "Evaluation of Rhythmic and Perceptual Skills" appears after Lesson 30.

PREPARATION FOR THE CHART

Note: The perfect fourth was introduced aurally on Charts 24 and 25. Now the class will read the interval on the staff.

1. Prepare the class by reviewing the intervals as presented in Lesson 25 by echo singing the intervals:

Teacher sings with hand signals	Class sings with hand signals
⊓ ⊓ ⊓ l s s l l s s m	major second, minor third
⊓ l ⊓ l s s m l l m	minor third, perfect fourth

Use other variations of the above activity.

INTRODUCE THE CHART

1. Point to the hand signals for *mi* on the chart. Sing the *mi* with hand signals and move to the *la* and sing the tone syllable. Repeat

Two-hand Singing

this activity several times, slowly. Be sure the class is able to hear the interval of the perfect fourth (*mi–la*).
2. Sing various patterns using *mi* and *la*.
3. Ask the class to explain the numbers *3* and *6* on the chart. (If necessary, review the vertical scale in Lesson 17.)
4. Tell the class that if *mi* is around a line, *la* will be two spaces above *mi* or in the space above *sol*. The same will apply to the *mi* in a space. The *la* would then be two lines above *mi* or around the line above *sol*.
5. Choose a student to lead the class while tapping several rhythm patterns on the chart with hand signals, using only one of the staves.

ADDITIONAL ACTIVITIES

1. Divide the class. Group 1 will follow the hand signals you give with your left hand; Group 2 will follow the hand signals you

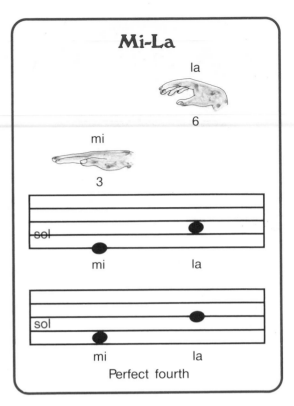

give with your right hand. Each group must sustain the tone as long as the hand signal remains the same; for example:

Left hand: s————l m l s m

Right hand: s l m m————

Note: Move slowly from one interval to another. This activity is called two-hand singing. As the class becomes more confident, do the above activity to various rhythm patterns:

Left hand: ⊓ l ⊓ l
m m l m m l ——————

Right hand: ⊓ l ⊓ l l
m ——————— l l m m m l

2. Ask for volunteers to lead the class in two-hand singing. Be sure to observe the spatial relationships of the intervals.
3. Proceed to the next chart.

Bobwhite

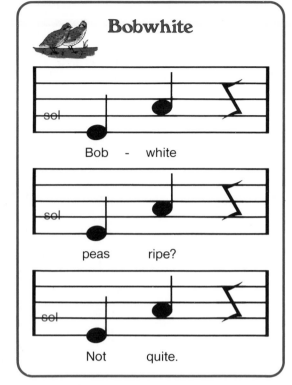

Bobwhite

Bob - white

peas ripe?

Not quite.

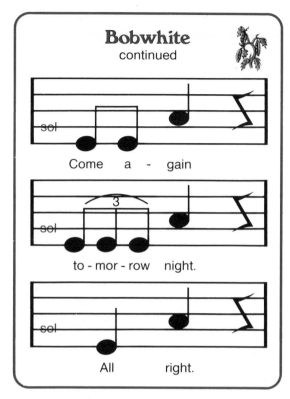

Bobwhite
continued

Come a - gain

3
to - mor - row night.

All right.

PREPARATION FOR THE CHARTS

1. Sing various patterns with hand singing, using *sol–la–mi.* The class will echo with hand signals:

```
    ⌐ 
 |  ⌐⌐ | |
 s  l l s m
 ⌐⌐ ⌐⌐ | |
 s s l l m l
```

2. Tell the class to listen carefully with inner hearing while you make the hand signals for the first two measures of "French Cathedrals" without singing:

```
 ⌐⌐ |  ⌐⌐ |
 s  l  m s l  m
```

Can the students identify the song? Sing the first two measures with the class, using hand signals.

3. Repeat this activity with "Ring Around the Rosy":

```
 ⌐⌐ ⌐⌐ | |
 s s m l  s m
```

Note: When you come to the interval of the perfect fourth (mi–la *ascending or* la–mi *descending), stop and repeat the interval.*

4. Make the hand signals for *mi–la* or *la–mi* without singing. Ask the class to listen to the sound they hear inside. Have them sing the interval with hand signals. If the class is insecure, start the pattern on *sol* (*sol–la–mi*).

5. Sing *mi–la–mi–la* with hand signals for the class to echo. Sing various rhythm patterns with *la–mi* or *mi–la* for echo singing.

6. *Two-hand singing:* This activity was presented in the preceding lesson. It should be used many times during the school year. Establish the pitch on a **unison** note and then proceed to two parts, moving one hand at a time. Begin slowly and keep the patterns simple, frequently returning to a unison note; this will check the **tonality.**

INTRODUCE THE CHARTS

1. Read the words with the class, keeping the beat while moving from chart to chart. Tell the class that the bobwhite is a small bird usually found in the midwestern and eastern states. Children in the western states will be more familiar with the quail, which is a relative of the bobwhite. The bobwhite's call is a clear whistle that is a perfect fourth (*mi–la*) and sounds like "bob–white."

2. Read and clap the rhythm pattern of both charts. Ask the class how many syllables

the word *tomorrow* has. How many times do they have to clap? *3* Do they remember what to say for the triplet? *tri-ple-ti* Be sure they make the rest motion and keep the beat.

Note: This will be an introduction to three beats on a chart. All previous rhythmic experiences have been in duple time, two and four.

3. Say the words and step the beat. How many beats do they feel? *3*

Note: When stepping triple beats, it is sometimes helpful to say, "Step-tip-toe." This will emphasize the accent on the first beat and also provide an introduction to the waltz without calling it "dancing."

4. Establish the pitch for *sol.* Ask the class to sing *la,* then sing *mi.* Repeat this interval several times until the class can sing the perfect fourth unassisted.
5. Sing the entire song using hand signals and tone syllables.
6. Sing the song with words and hand signals.
7. Divide the class into two groups. Group 1 sings the question, and Group 2 sings the answer with hand signals.
8. Choose two students. Ask the first to sing the question and the second to answer with words and hand signals.

ADDITIONAL ACTIVITIES

1. The class should be encouraged to write music. This will combine listening, writing, reading, and singing activities to further develop and reinforce new learnings:

Teacher claps:

Class echoes:

Class claps and says:
ta — ta — | ta ti—ti ta —

Class writes:

Put the pattern on the chalkboard.
2. *Dictation for "Hey, Ho! Nobody Home":* draw a staff on the chalkboard and place *sol* on the second line:

Note: If the class members have individual music staves with cut-out notes and rests, it will be invaluable in the teaching of melodic skills.

Ask one student to show the correct position for *la* on the staff:

Sing *la* and make the rest motion, then sing *sol* and make the rest motion. What comes after *la?* Ask for a volunteer to add the rest. What comes after the rest? *sol* Ask other students to add a *sol,* and then another

rest. Continue with the remainder of the melodic pattern:

What is the name of the song? Sing what the class has written. The students will be delighted to find that they have written the first phrase of "Hey, Ho! Nobody Home." Sing the song and ask a small group to sing the melodic phrase they have just written as an ostinato.
3. This last activity can be used many times with song fragments to reinforce a particular interval or rhythm pattern.

EVALUATION OF RHYTHMIC AND PERCEPTUAL SKILLS

Aural and Visual Acuity and Perception

1. Can the class hear the interval of the perfect fourth while reading a chart or observing hand signals?
2. Can the students read the charts and recognize the perfect fourth?

Musical Development and Social Maturity

1. Can the students hear a melody and place the notes on the staff?
2. Are they becoming increasingly confident with musical notation?
3. Are an increasing number of students volunteering to take part in the musical activities of the class?

31 Sol-Mi-Do

Do

Do¹

Sol-Mi-Do

sol
5

mi
3

do
1

Note: Charts 31 and 32 combine to form a single concept, and therefore the "Evaluation of Rhythmic and Perceptual Skills" is presented at the end of Chart 32.

INTRODUCE THE CHART

1. Tell the class they have sung *do* many times, usually at the end of a song. Review some familiar songs. Stop the song just before the final note (*do*):
   - "Old MacDonald"—"ee–i–ee–i–(*o*)"
   - "Bingo"—"and Bingo was his (*name–o*)"
   - "Skip to My Lou"—"Skip to my Lou my (*dar–ling*)"

2. The hand signal for *do* is a strongly clenched fist.
   Note: The tone syllable do *is the home tone or key syllable of many songs, and most children's songs are written in a major key.*

3. Use the hand signals on the chart and have the class sing *sol–mi–do* with hand signals, holding each syllable for four beats.

   Note: Encourage the students to sing each note with adequate breath support. When singing sol *and* do, *tell the class to make their mouths like "O's," wide enough to insert three fingers between their teeth. When singing* mi, *have them smile with their lips pulled back and their jaws relaxed.*

4. Use the hand signals on the chart and have the class sing *sol–mi–do* slowly with hand signals.

5. Repeat the above activity and sing *5–3–1*, with hand signals. Ask the class to explain why *do* is called *1*. Review the vertical scale to illustrate the position of *do* on the numerical scale.

6. Create various rhythm patterns on the chart with hand signals.

Teacher sings	Class echoes with hand signals
I ⊓ I I s mm d d	I ⊓ I I s mm d d
⊓ I ⊓ I dd m ss m	⊓ I ⊓ I dd m ss m

Note: These patterns can be as complex as the class is capable of doing. Start slowly and progress to the more difficult patterns. You will find that the students will have more success singing the descending sol–do *than singing the ascending* do–sol.

7. Establish the pitch for *sol.* Create various rhythm patterns on the chart but *do not* sing. The class will sing the patterns you indicate with hand signals:

Teacher	Class sings with hand signals
I I ⊓ I s m dd d	I I ⊓ I s m dd d
⊓ I ⊓ I s m d d md	⊓ I ⊓ I s m d s md

As the class becomes more confident, use two-measure patterns such as:

I ⊓ I I | I 𝄽 I 𝄽
s mm d d | m s

Ask one of the students to lead the class in this activity.

8. Use your hand to illustrate the five lines of the staff. Establish the position of *sol* and have volunteers find *mi,* and then *do.* Vary the position of *sol.* Sing the intervals as they are identified. Remember, if *sol* is around a line, *mi* will be around the line below *sol* and *do* will be around the line below *mi.* Use the spaces to show this relationship.
9. Proceed to the next chart.

Old Woman

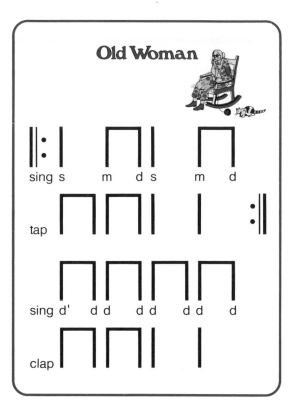

OLD WOMAN

American Folk Song

1. Old Wo-man, old wo-man, Are you fond of card - ing?

Old wo-man, old wo-man, Are you fond of card - ing?

Speak a lit - tle loud - er, sir! I'm ver - y hard of hear - ing.

2. Old woman, old woman,
   Are you fond of spinning? (*Repeat*)
   Speak a little louder, sir!
   I'm very hard of hearing.

3. Old woman, old woman,
   will you darn my stocking? (*Repeat*)
   Speak a little louder, sir!
   I'm very hard of hearing.

4. Old woman, old woman,
   Will you let me court you? (*Repeat*)
   Speak a little louder, sir!
   I just begin to hear you.

5. Old woman, old woman,
   Don't you want to marry me? (*Repeat*)
   Oh, my goodness gracious me!
   I think that now I hear you.

PREPARATION FOR THE CHART

1. Teach the song (all verses).
2. Sing the song, using previous rhythmic experiences.

INTRODUCE THE CHART

1. Choose one student to clap the rhythm pattern on the chart with rhythm syllables. Be certain to observe the repeat signs.
2. Choose another student to sing the first line of the chart with hand signals. The class will tap the second line. Let the student who sings the first line establish the pitch for *sol*.
3. Read and sing the entire chart with tone syllables, hand signals, tapping, and clapping. Observe the repeat signs.

Note: When reading the high do¹, observe the spatial relationship of the interval. Tell the class they are singing an octave.

- Discuss the prefix *octa-*.
- How many arms does an octopus have? *8*
- How many sides does an octagon have? *8*
- How many steps on the vertical scale from *do* to *do¹*? *8*

4. Use flash cards for inner hearing with the chart:

feel   step   instruments

Choose individuals to sing Lines 1 and 3 and have the class follow the directions on the flash cards for Lines 2 and 4.

5. Sing the song with words and hand signals.
6. After the class has learned all the verses, divide them into two groups—one to sing the questions (first two lines), and the other to sing the part of the old woman. Use hand signals and rhythmic activities.

ADDITIONAL ACTIVITIES

1. *Similarities and Differences:* Which phrases are alike? Make a picture of the melody, first in the air with arm movements, then on paper:

Phrase 1:   Phrase 2:

Phrase 3:

The form can also be shown with letters or geometric shapes:

A   A   B   ●   ●   ▲

2. **Instruments:** Read and play the pattern on the chart with rhythm instruments:

- Lines 1 and 2—woodblock or sticks
- Lines 3 and 4—tambourine or drum

Pass out the *C–E–G* and high *C* resonator bells. Let the students discover which bells will play the melody.

- "Old woman"   *G–E–C*
- "Speak a little louder..."   *C¹–C–C–C–C–C*

This activity can also be performed on the recorder, song flute, or song bells.

Note: The notes C–E–G–C¹ will be closest to the class's vocal range.

EVALUATION OF RHYTHMIC AND PERCEPTUAL SKILLS

Aural Acuity and Perception

1. Can the students hear and sing the descending major third (*mi–do*)?
2. Can they hear the similarities and differences in a melody?
3. Can they hear and recognize the high *do* (*do¹*)?

Visual Acuity and Perception

1. Can the students recognize the *do* on the musical staff?
2. Can they read the pattern on the chart while singing or playing an instrument?

Musical Development and Social Maturity

1. Can the students successfully relate previous musical learnings to a familiar song?
2. Can they approach and perform a new song with little or no assistance from the teacher?

Mystery Songs

1. WE'RE GOING 'ROUND THE MOUNTAIN

American Singing Game

1. We're go-ing 'round the mount-ain,

two by two, We're go-ing 'round the

mount-ain, two by two, We're

go -ing 'round the mount-ain, two by

two, So rise, Sal-ly, rise.

2. Let's see you make a motion, two by two, (*3 times*)
So rise, Sally, rise.

3. That's a mighty fine motion, two by two, (*3 times*)
So rise, Sally, rise.

4. Let's see you make another, two by two, (*3 times*)
So rise, Sally, rise.

Note: The "Evaluation of Rhythmic and Perceptual Skills" appears at the end of Lesson 34.

PREPARATION FOR THE CHART

We're Going 'Round the Mountain

1. Teach the song (all verses).
2. Sing the song and use previous rhythmic experiences.
3. Sing the song and create a rhythmic ostinato, such as:

- slap knees
- clap
- finger snap right hand
- finger snap left hand

Begin the ostinato on the first beat, not the anacrusis. Encourage individual students to create their own ostinato, using different sounds:

- clap
- tap desk
- pat knees
- snap fingers

The class will then use this ostinato and sing the song.

Love Somebody

1. Teach the song. There are many verses to this song not given here.
2. Sing the song and use previous rhythmic experiences:

- Sing Measure 1 with hand signals—clap Measure 2

- Sing Measure 3 with hand signals—step Measure 4

- Sing Measure 5 with hand signals—feel Measure 6

- Sing and step the rhythm pattern for Measures 7—8.

Repeat the above activity for the refrain.

2. LOVE SOMEBODY

U.S. Folk Song

Love some-bod-y, yes I do, Love some-bod-y, yes I do,

Love some-bod-y, yes I do, Love some-bod-y but I won't tell who.

Refrain

Love some-bod-y, yes I do, Love some-bod-y, yes I do,

Love some-bod-y, yes I do, And I hope some-bod-y loves me too.

3. ROLL OVER

Traditional

1. There were ten in the bed and the lit-tle one said, "Roll o-ver, Roll
2. There were nine . . .

o-ver," So they all rolled o-ver and one fell out. There was

one in the bed so the lit-tle one said, "Good night, Good night."

Note: The class will notice the sixteenth notes, which were introduced on Chart 20, by having to make four quick steps to the beat. If the class wishes to know the rhythm syllables for the sixteenth-note pattern, tell them to say "ti-di-ti-di" on one beat. The sixteenth note will be developed further on succeeding charts.

Roll Over

1. Teach the song, singing all ten verses, from "ten in the bed" through "one in the bed."

Note: Remember that repetition offers an opportunity to the insecure or nonparticipating student who often is listening and waiting to become a part of the song. A fun song such

as "Roll Over" may give such a student the opportunity and time to develop a positive attitude toward him or herself in relationship to music.

2. Sing the song and use previous rhythmic experiences. Be aware of the anacrusis.
3. Choose ten students and number them from ten to one. The entire class will sing the song while clapping the pattern, and each numbered student will sing "Roll Over" using hand signals for *sol–mi–do*. The last student (Number 1) will sing "Good night" on *mi–do*.
4. Sing the song, clap the pattern, and use hand signals for "Roll over" (*sol–mi–do*) and "Good night" (*mi–do*).

INTRODUCE THE CHART

1. Ask a volunteer to choose one line on the chart and clap the rhythm pattern. Can the class identify the pattern by holding up one, two, or three fingers?
2. Ask for volunteers to sing a line of the chart with hand signals. Can the class identify the song? Sing the entire song.
3. Continue through the entire chart. The student who correctly identifies the song may lead the class while they sing.

OTHER SONGS TO USE

- "Skip to my Lou"

  m m d d   d m m m s

- "Paw Paw Patch"

  d d d d   d m s s m d

- "Fooba Wooba John"

  d d m m m s

ADDITIONAL ACTIVITIES

1. Use individual charts or staff paper for dictation. Establish the position for *sol* and *do* (third line, fourth space, and so on):

Teacher sings with hand signals	Class echoes, then writes

| | ⊓ |	
s m s m d	

⊓ | ⊓ |	
d m s s m d	

2. Establish the pitch for *sol* or *do.* Make the hand signals for a melodic pattern but *do not* sing. The class will sing the tone syllables with hand signals.

3. Make flash cards of various melodic patterns using *sol–mi–do:*

| ≀ ⊓ |	⊓ | ⊓ |	| ⊓ ⊓ |
s m m d	d m s m m d	s m m s s d

Establish the starting pitch. Hold up a flash card. The class will sing the pattern with hand signals.

Note: When the students are confident with this activity, ask individuals to sing the flash cards. Let each student establish his or her own pitch. This will vary with each individual.

4. *Intervals:* This activity can be quite a challenge to the class, if they are thoroughly confident singing the intervals learned thus far. You may need the assistance of your music specialist, but there can be astounding results.

Teacher sings on "loo" with hand signals	Class sings with hand signals
s m s m G E G E	*sol–mi,* minor third
l m l m A E A E	*la–mi,* perfect fourth
s d s d G C G C	*sol–do,* perfect fifth

Note: This activity can also be done on the piano, bells, or recorder.

5. Proceed to the next chart.

The Triad

The Triad

Sing
and
Listen

PREPARATION FOR THE CHART

A **chord** is formed by sounding groups of tones simultaneously. A **triad** is a chord formed by sounding three tones simultaneously.

Note: A discussion of prefixes will clarify the concept of the triad:

> *tri*—tricycle (three wheels)
> triangle (three-sided figure)
> triad (three tones)

The **tonic** chord is a triad using *sol—mi—do* and is most commonly heard in Western music. Most songs begin and end on one of the tones of the tonic chord. The tonic chord is often called the *key chord,* because it is built on *do,* which establishes the key in which the song is to be performed.

INTRODUCE THE CHART

1. Divide the class into three groups, and establish the pitch for *sol.*

   - The entire class sings *sol.*
   - Group 1 sings *sol* and continues to sing with good breath support, taking a breath whenever necessary.

   - Give the hand signal for *mi.* Groups 2 and 3 sing *mi* while Group 1 continues to sing *sol.*
   - Give the hand signal for *do* to Group 3; each group continues singing its note.

2. Tell the class they are singing a chord or triad. Do the above activity several times. When the class hears the chord for the first time, they are amazed.

   Note: The tendency will be to oversing (shout) at first. Encourage the class to sing the triad softly, with a beautiful tone—jaws relaxed and lips formed properly for each syllable.

3. Divide the class into three groups. Build the triad on "loo," starting with *sol,* then *mi,* and finally *do.* Start the triad softly and gradually get louder (crescendo ◁). You will find that many students will alter the pitch upward as they get louder. Begin the crescendo gradually. If the pitch begins to change, decrescendo (▷) until the class can hear the chord.

4. Build the chord on "loo" and when the pitch is established, give a signal (clap, tap the desk, or some other sign) to stop singing.

At a given signal, sing the chord again. Repeat this activity several times, using different dynamics.

EVALUATION OF RHYTHMIC AND PERCEPTUAL SKILLS

Aural Acuity and Perception

1. Can the students hear the descending thirds that are used in a triad?
2. Can they hear and reproduce a major chord?
3. Can they recognize the triad within a familiar song?

Visual Acuity and Perception

1. Can the students recognize the *sol—mi—do* on the musical staff?
2. Can they establish the position of *sol—mi—do* on paper or individual charts?

Sing Sol–Mi–Do

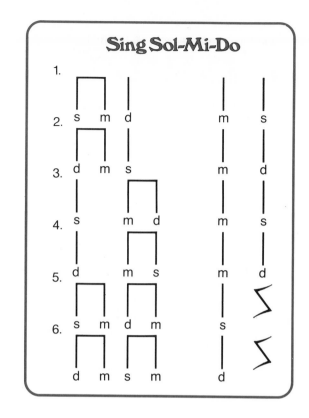

Note: Charts 35 and 36 reinforce the sol–mi–do. *The "Evaluation of Rhythmic and Perceptual Skills" will follow Chart 36.*

INTRODUCE THE CHART

1. Clap the rhythm pattern, step the beat, and read the rhythm syllables. Move from line to line without losing the beat.
2. Clap the beat, read and step the rhythm pattern.
3. Step the beat, clap and read the pattern, turn slightly to the right at the end of the first line (phrase), turn to the left at the end of the second phrase, and so on, continuing through the chart.
4. Read the rhythm symbols and make the hand signals for the syllables without singing. Keep the beat as you move from line to line.

Note: Take special note of the spatial relationships of the intervals while doing the above activity.

5. Read and sing the tone syllables with hand signals. Begin this activity slowly at first, then increase the **tempo.**
6. Divide the class. Group 1 sings the left side of the chart. Group 2 sings the right side. Keep the beat as the groups alternate singing.
7. Group 1 sings Line 1, Group 2 sings Line 2. Continue through the chart, alternating between the two groups.
8. Choose individuals to sing Activities 6 and 7 using hand signals.

ADDITIONAL ACTIVITIES

1. Create words to the pattern and sing the chart with hand signals.

```
┌──┐  │     │ │
s  m  d     m  s
How are you?  I'm fine.
┌──┐  │     │ │
d  m  s     m  d
Can you play?  Not now.
```

Continue through the entire chart, letting the class create their own conversation to fit the rhythm pattern.

2. Choose individual students to clap a pattern of four beats. Ask the class to echo and write the pattern on a piece of paper. Let each student write the syllables, using letter names, under the rhythm symbols. Give each student an opportunity to sing his or her pattern to the class.

Note: Some of the students will need assistance in establishing the pitch (sol or do). As the class becomes more confident, extend the pattern to two or more measures.

3. Create words to the original melodic patterns.

```
⊓    ⊓  |  |        |  ⸴ | |
s  m  d  d  m  s      |     s m
```
Do you like to play ball?   Yes, I do.

Note: This activity can be developed into quite a creative experience, both musically and in language arts. As the students sing their original melodies, let them discover that do at the end of the melodic pattern gives a feeling of finality, much as a period does at the end of a sentence. The syllables of the words must fit the rhythmic pattern. Not everyone in the class will be successful with this activity. Choose some of the original songs to put on a chart for the class to sing. Use different subject areas as themes, such as the weather, social studies, or language arts.

4. Divide the class into two groups.

Group 1	Group 2
Claps ostinato softly	Sings the chart with hand signals
⏐ ⏐ ⊓ ⏐	
Sings the chart with hand signals	Steps an ostinato
	⊓ ⏐ ⏐ ⏐
Sings *sol* throughout	Sings the chart
♩ ♩	
s s	
Sings the chart	Sings *sol–do* throughout
	♩ ♩
	s d

Note: The above activities can be done by individual students. The singing should be done with a beautiful tone and hand signals. This type of activity can be used many times during the school year and is not necessarily limited to the music class.

5. Establish the pitch for *sol*. Make the hand signals for *sol–mi–do,* using various rhythm patterns, but *do not* sing.

Teacher or leader				Class sings with hand signals			
⏐	⏐ ⊓ ⏐			⏐	⏐ ⊓ ⏐		
s	m d d s			s	m d d s		
⊓ ⏐ ⏐	⏐			⊓ ⏐ ⏐	⏐		
d d m s	s			d d m s	s		

This activity can also be used for dictation. After the class echoes the pattern, place the notes on the staff, either individual staff charts, or on a piece of paper.

6. Make flash cards of various melodic patterns using *sol–mi–do.* Show the card and have the class sing it using hand signals. Give each student an opportunity to sing a card individually.

Note: If you keep the beat as you move from student to student, you will create a feeling of excitement that will help the individual student who feels insecure or shy about singing a solo. You may have to reinforce the starting pitch.

7. Proceed to the next chart.

Question • Answer

Question • Answer

Note: This chart is a preparation for creative activities involving rhythm and melody. This may sound highly technical to the classroom teacher with little training in music, but students who have performed the previous rhythmic and melodic activities will thoroughly enjoy composing their own patterns. You will find that students have a tendency to echo the pattern they have just heard when beginning this activity, but encourage them to create their own patterns. They will soon surprise you.

PREPARATION FOR THE CHART

1. *Creative Rhythmic Activity:* Tell the class they will be composing their own rhythm patterns after the class echoes the teacher. Choose individuals to create a pattern:

Teacher claps	Class echoes	One student claps

Put a pattern on the board, your own or one of the student's:

Teacher claps A

A. | | ⊓ |

One student claps B

B. ⊓ | | ⊓ |

Teacher and class clap A

A. | | ⊓ |

One student claps C, and so on

C. | ⸸ ⊓ |

Move around the room so that each student has an opportunity to create a pattern,

keeping the beat. This activity will prepare the class for **rondo** form: A–B–A–C–A, and so on.

2. *Creative Melodic Activity:*

Teacher sings with hand signals	Class echoes	One student sings
					s s s m							s s s m					s m s m
	⊓			s l l s m		⊓	m	s l l s m		⊓			s m m d d

Teacher moves from student to student, asking a musical question with hand signals, which is answered by the student, who also uses hand signals. If the question has four beats, the answer should have four beats:

Teacher	Student
I I I 𝄽	I I I 𝄽
d m s	s m d
How are you?	I am fine.

⌐ ⌐I I	I II 𝄽
s s I I s m	s I s
Do you have a pencil?	Yes, I do.

Note: The answer will not always end on do (home tone). As the class becomes more confident, they will create longer patterns and use different melodic combinations.

INTRODUCE THE CHART

1. Clap the rhythm pattern of the first line with rhythm syllables. How many beats does each measure have? 2
2. Ask one student to clap the rhythm pattern of the second line. What happens to the last beat? Tell the student to clap any pattern he or she wishes to complete the phrase. What will it be? 𝄽, I, ⌐, ⌐⌐
3. Ask the class to clap the second line using the previous rhythm pattern.
4. Continue through the chart, letting one student create the final beat.
5. Establish the pitch for *do*. Sing the first line of the chart with the class, using hand signals.
6. Divide the class. One group sings the question, the other group sings the answer of the first line.
7. Choose a student to sing the question and another to sing the answer of the first line, using hand signals.

8. Put the second line of the chart on the board. Sing the first measure with the class. Choose one student to sing the answer, using any syllable he or she wishes, with the correct hand signals. Put the tone symbol on the chalkboard under the rhythm symbol.
9. Continue throughout the entire chart, creating an "original" melodic pattern.
10. Divide the class. One group sings the question, the other sings the answer, using the "original" rhythmic and melodic pattern.
11. Ask two students to sing the entire chart with hand signals and tone syllables.
12. To encourage the creative student, ask for volunteers to create a different ending for each phrase. The class sings the question, and one student sings the answer, creating his or her own melody.

ADDITIONAL ACTIVITIES

1. Make up words to the conversation; for example:

| I I | I I |
| Hel—lo. | Hel—lo. |

| ⌐ I | ⌐ I |
| How are you? | I am fine. |

| ⌐ I | I I |
| Can you play? | Not now. |

| I ⌐ | ⌐ I ⌐ |
| I'll see you. | Thanks for call—ing. |

2. Create another conversation using four beats to a measure. Put the pattern on the chalkboard using tone syllables. Use the syllables *sol—mi—do* at first; later, add *la*.

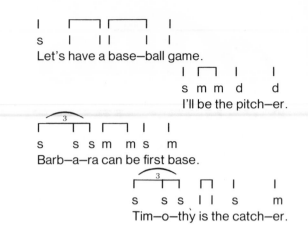

I ⌐ ⌐ I
s I I I I I
Let's have a base—ball game.

I ⌐ I I
s m m d   d
I'll be the pitch—er.

³
⌐⌐ ⌐ I I
s   s s m m s m
Barb—a—ra can be first base.

³
⌐ ⌐ I I
s s s I I s   m
Tim—o—thy is the catch—er.

EVALUATION OF RHYTHMIC AND PERCEPTUAL SKILLS

Aural and Visual Acuity and Perception

1. Can the students read and hear the perfect fifth (*sol—do, do—sol*)?
2. Can they read the musical symbols on the chart and sing the melodic phrase?
3. Can the students recognize the perfect fifth?

Musical Development and Social Maturity

1. Can the students create original rhythmic and melodic patterns?
2. Can they perform their original patterns with confidence?
3. Can the students fit the syllabication of a word to a rhythm pattern?
4. Can they create musical conversations in two-measure and four-measure phrases?
5. Can they concentrate on longer rhythmic and melodic phrases?
6. Are more students volunteering to create a rhythmic or melodic pattern?

Surprise Symphony

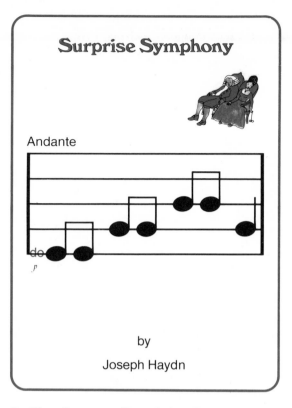

Surprise Symphony

Andante

by

Joseph Haydn

Note: In order to use this chart you will need to play a recording of Haydn's "Surprise Symphony." This can be obtained through your music department. Review Chart 20. If you wish to tell the class more about Joseph Haydn, Lillian Baldwin's Music for Young Listeners, Blue Book *(Silver Burdett) is invaluable.*

PREPARATION FOR THE CHART.

1. Recall the story of "Papa" Haydn given in Lesson 20.
2. Tell the class about the "Surprise Symphony."

Joseph Haydn's orchestra often played for guests after dinner. The ladies would come to the concert in their powdered wigs and hooped skirts and the gentlemen in their knee breeches and buckled shoes. Perhaps they ate too much dinner, or they didn't know how to listen to good music, so they would often sleep through the concert. This is what made Haydn decide to play a joke.

Andante (ahn–dahn'–tā) means moderately slow, just right for someone to take a little nap. This is where Haydn decided to surprise everyone. The music starts softly and gently, and just when Haydn figured everyone would be nodding, every instrument in the orchestra plays as loudly as it can on a chord. (Remember the chord?—several notes played or sung at the same time.)

"There," said Haydn, with a twinkle in his eye. "That should wake them up," He was not mistaken. Even though there were no more loud chords, everyone wanted to stay awake, just in case.

3. Play the recording of the *Andante* to the "Surprise Symphony." Can the class tell why this composition is called the "Surprise Symphony"?

Note: You may wish to play more of the record, depending upon the attention span of your class.

INTRODUCE THE CHART

1. Ask the class to read the music on the chart and hear the melody in their heads. Use hand signals.
2. Establish the pitch for *do*. Ask the class to sing the chart with hand signals.
3. Ask the class where they have heard this melody before. Who is the composer?
4. Play the record again. Ask the class to raise

their hands or make the hand signals every time they hear the opening theme:

⊓ ⊓ ⊓ |
d d m m s s m

5. Ask the students if the melody on the recording is *always* exactly the same.

- Can they recognize the theme when there is another melody playing at the same time?
- Can they recognize the theme when the rhythm pattern changes?

♫♫ ♫♫ ♫♫ ♫♫
d d d d m m m m s s s s m m m m

6. Is the theme always played softly (*p*)?

ADDITIONAL ACTIVITIES

1. Encourage the students to do further research on the life and times of Joseph Haydn:

- type of dress
- housing—castles and palaces
- kings and queens

Have the class compare the life of George Washington and Joseph Haydn.
2. Tell the class that the **minuet** was a popular dance of the period, which they might like to perform.

EVALUATION OF RHYTHMIC AND PERCEPTUAL SKILLS

Aural Acuity and Perception

Are the students able to listen to a composition and discover similarities and differences such as

- recurring themes?
- the melody, played higher or lower?
- alterations in rhythmic pattern?

Musical Development

Are the students demonstrating an increasing enjoyment while listening to a composition?

The Town Crier

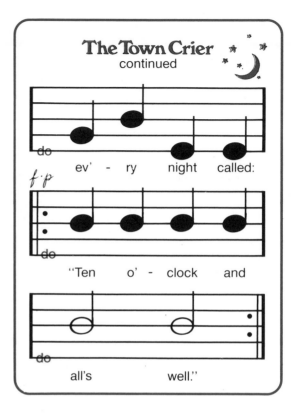

The Town Crier

do — Long   a - go   the

do — old   town   cri - er

do — walked   the   streets   and

The Town Crier continued

do — ev' - ry   night   called:

f · p

do — "Ten   o' - clock   and

do — all's   well."

PREPARATION FOR THE CHARTS

Tell the class that before we had radio, telephone, television, newspapers, and electric clocks the villages had *town criers.* The town criers walked through the town, ringing a large bell and telling everyone the news and the time of day or night by calling out at intervals. The town criers found that if they sang the time, their voices carried farther and sounded more interesting. The bell would help them keep the beat as they walked, and it announced to everyone that the crier was coming.

INTRODUCE THE CHARTS

1. Read the two charts for this lesson with hand signals and put the melody inside (inner hearing). On what tone syllable does the song begin? *mi* Move from one chart to the other without losing the beat.

2. Step the beat and make the hand signals for both charts. How many steps did the class take on the last measure? *4* How many beats did each note get in the last measure? *2*

3. Tell the class the last two notes are half notes. Each note gets two beats and is twice as long as a quarter note (l–ta). The rhythm syllables are "ta–a, ta–a," with a clap for the first beat and a squeeze for the second beat.

4. Ask one student to establish the pitch for *sol;* this will be a relative pitch. Ask another student or the class to sing *mi.* This is the starting tone.

5. Establish the beat by saying, "one, two, ready, sing."

   - Step the beat.
   - Sing the charts with tone syllables and hand signals.
   - Observe the repeat signs (‖: :‖).

6. Ask the class what the *f* and *p* mean on the last phrase. *Sing the last phrase loudly*—f; *sing the repeat softly*—p. Tell the students the town crier is walking away and his voice is getting softer.

7. Read the words with the class.

   - Sing the chart with words and hand signals.
   - Step the beat.
   - Observe the dynamics (*f–p*).
   - Observe the repeat signs (‖: :‖).

ADDITIONAL ACTIVITIES

1. Divide the class into two groups. Group 1 steps the beat (♩ ♩ ♩ ♩) and Group 2 steps only the half notes (♩ ♩).

2. Using the same activity, Group 1 sings the songs with words and hand signals, while Group 2 sings *sol–do* or "ding-dong," using the half note (ding-dong—♩ ♩).

3. Form two circles, one inside the other. The outer circle walks the beat while singing the song. The inner circle walks the half notes, singing "ding-dong" on *sol–do*. Both groups should use hand signals while singing.

4. Draw three lines on the floor about a foot apart (*sol–mi–do*). Choose one student to step the melody while the class sings the song.

```
sol ————×———————×————
mi  —×——×——×——×——————
do  ————————×—————×——
```

Note: This activity will provide a welcome break in the day when the class is restless or needs a change of pace. Let each student decide whether the song begins on a line or space.

5. Pass out resonator bells to form a major triad. For example:

C–E–G   F–A–C   G–B–D

*Note: Other triads will need a **sharp** (♯) or flat (♭).*

Let the students with the bells create an ostinato while the rest of the class sings the song. Ask the students with bells to play the major triad on the first beat of each measure. Later, let them create a rhythm pattern to play on the bells as an accompaniment.

EVALUATION OF RHYTHMIC AND PERCEPTUAL SKILLS

Note: The preceding charts emphasized the importance of the tone syllable do. *In Western music and in many children's songs, the* do *is often the final note, giving a feeling of finality at the end of the song.*

Psychomotor Development and Perception

Is the class becoming increasingly confident while performing rhythmic activities such as

- walking or stepping the beat in a relaxed manner?
- combining integrated activities?

Aural Acuity and Perception

1. Can the students read and hear the interval of the perfect fifth (*sol–do, do–sol*) and major third (*mi–do, do–mi*)?
2. Can they differentiate notes of varying lengths, for example, ♩ ⊓ ♩ ?
3. Are they becoming increasingly aware of various intervals, such as *sol–la, sol–mi, la–sol, la–mi*?

Visual Acuity and Perception

1. Can the students read a chart and perform various activities from simple to complex, such as

- reading the pattern?
- singing the syllables?
- observing the repeat signs (‖: :‖)?
- observing dynamic markings (*f–p*)?

2. Can they recognize and perform various intervals on the chart?

39
A New Note–Re

Re

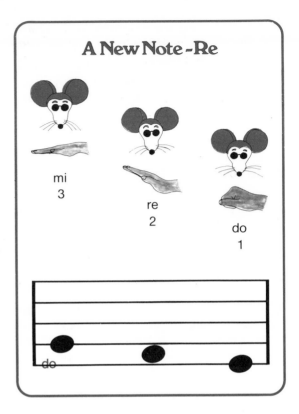

A New Note –Re

mi
3

re
2

do
1

do

THREE BLIND MICE

Traditional Round

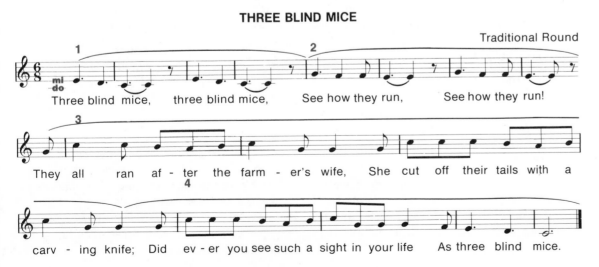

mi
do

Three blind mice, three blind mice, See how they run, See how they run!

They all ran af - ter the farm - er's wife, She cut off their tails with a

carv - ing knife; Did ev - er you see such a sight in your life As three blind mice.

Note: The next four charts, 39, 40, 41, and 42, teach the interval of the major second. The "Evaluation of Rhythmic and Perceptual Skills" for these charts appears at the end of Lesson 42.

PREPARATION FOR THE CHART

1. Teach the song.
2. Clap the rhythm pattern of the song as a mystery song. Although the **time signature** is in $\frac{6}{8}$, clap the pattern with the beat in two:

   ♩. ♩. | ♫ ♫
   1   2 | 1   2

3. Sing the song and step or walk the beat.

4. Sing the song and use previous rhythmic experiences (refer to Chart 11). Use flash cards for inner hearing.

*Note: The notation on the chart differs from the song shown here because of the use of **ledger lines**, which will be introduced on a later chart.*

INTRODUCE THE CHART

1. Hold your hand over the hand signal for *mi* on the chart. Sing *mi* with the class with hand signals.
2. Point to the *re* on the chart. Tilt your hand so it points upward. Sing *re* with the class.
3. Make the hand signal for the *do* on the chart and sing it with the class.
4. Repeat these activities, moving from one syllable to another in various patterns.
5. Use the hand and fingers to establish the position of *re* in relationship to *mi* and *do*.

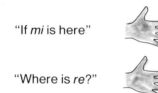

"If *mi* is here"

"Where is *re*?"

Later, use your hand to show the position of *re* in relationship to *sol* and *la,* using both lines and spaces.

6. Point to the numbers on the chart and ask the class what interval they sing from *mi* to *re*. major second What is the interval from *re* to *do*? major second How can they tell if the second is major or minor? Review Lesson 24 with a piano keyboard or resonator bells.

OTHER SONGS TO USE

- "Are You Sleeping?"
  d r m d | d r m d

- Yankee Doodle"
  d d r m | d m r (s₁)

- "Polly Wolly Doodle"
  d r | m m d d d r | m m d

Note: These are song fragments that use do–re–mi in varying patterns. Use only the melodic fragments that reinforce the use of re.

ADDITIONAL ACTIVITIES

*Note: The class has now learned the entire **pentatonic** scale (do, re, mi, sol, la). There are many songs written in the pentatonic, starting on low* sol (s₁) *and using low* la (l₁). *These songs can be taught by rote.*

1. Choose five students to represent the pentatonic scale, giving each one a tone syllable. This activity is sometimes called the "human organ." The high *do* (d¹) can also be used.

Have each student hold a flash card of his or her tone syllable. Establish the pitch—either *sol* or *do*. As you point to the syllables, the class sings with hand signals. Move slowly from interval to interval. Ask a student to lead this activity.

Note: This activity can be accomplished successfully only if the class is confident with the intervals that have been presented. The intervals can be sung with tone syllables or interval names (minor third, major second, and so on).

2. The concept of larger instruments having lower voices can be demonstrated by choosing the tallest student to be low *do* and the smallest student to represent high *do¹*.

3. Sing various patterns using notes of the pentatonic scale with hand signals. Class echoes:

Teacher or leader	Class echoes
l l ⌐ l	l l ⌐ l
s s m r d	s s m r d
l l l ⸜	l l l ⸜
m r d	m r d

4. Use hand signals but *do not* sing. Then, have the class sing the tone syllables with hand signals.
5. Make flash cards of various melodic patterns using *re*. Establish the pitch:

Hold up the card. Class sings with hand signals. Then, move from student to student and let individuals sing the patterns on the flash cards.

6. Put the musical staff on the chalkboard, but have the class use individual charts. Establish where the beginning note will be.

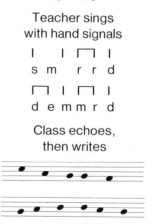

Teacher sings
with hand signals

l l ⌐ l
s m r r d

⌐ l ⌐ l
d e m m r d

Class echoes,
then writes

Choose individual students to come to the board and write the melodic pattern. This will give the class members an opportunity to correct their own mistakes.

7. Divide the class into two, three, or four groups and sing the song as a round.
8. Proceed to Chart 40.

Mystery Songs

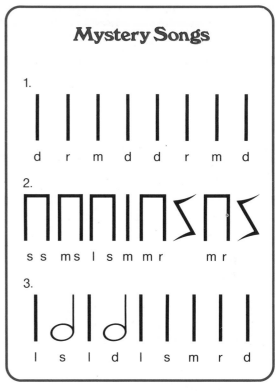

Mystery Songs

1.

d r m d d r m d

2.

s s m s l s m m r m r

3.

l s l d l s m r d

1. ARE YOU SLEEPING?

French Round

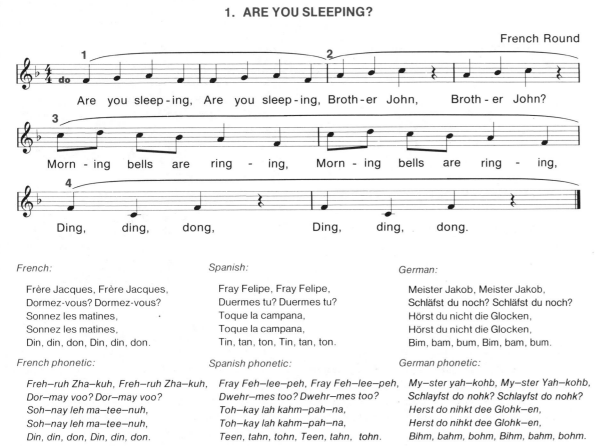

Are you sleep-ing, Are you sleep-ing, Broth-er John, Broth-er John?

Morn - ing bells are ring - ing, Morn - ing bells are ring - ing,

Ding, ding, dong, Ding, ding, dong.

French:

Frère Jacques, Frère Jacques,
Dormez-vous? Dormez-vous?
Sonnez les matines,
Sonnez les matines,
Din, din, don, Din, din, don.

French phonetic:

Freh–ruh Zha–kuh, Freh–ruh Zha–kuh,
Dor–may voo? Dor–may voo?
Soh–nay leh ma–tee–nuh,
Soh–nay leh ma–tee–nuh,
Din, din, don, Din, din, don.

Spanish:

Fray Felipe, Fray Felipe,
Duermes tu? Duermes tu?
Toque la campana,
Toque la campana,
Tin, tan, ton, Tin, tan, ton.

Spanish phonetic:

Fray Feh–lee–peh, Fray Feh–lee–peh,
Dwehr–mes too? Dwehr–mes too?
Toh–kay lah kahm–pah–na,
Toh–kay lah kahm–pah–na,
Teen, tahn, tohn, Teen, tahn, tohn.

German:

Meister Jakob, Meister Jakob,
Schläfst du noch? Schläfst du noch?
Hörst du nicht die Glocken,
Hörst du nicht die Glocken,
Bim, bam, bum, Bim, bam, bum.

German phonetic:

My–ster yah–kohb, My–ster Yah–kohb,
Schlayfst do nohk? Schlayfst do nohk?
Herst do nihkt dee Glohk–en,
Herst do nihkt dee Glohk–en,
Bihm, bahm, bohm, Bihm, bahm, bohm.

PREPARATION FOR THE CHART

Are You Sleeping?

1. Teach the song. Your class might be interested in learning the song in different languages.
2. Sing the song, using previous rhythmic experiences.
3. Sing the song with a melodic ostinato (for example, *sol–do* on the first and third beats).
4. Sing the song as a round in two, three, or four parts, depending upon the musical abilities of your class.
5. Sing the song as a round, step the beat, and turn the phrases.

2. CAMPTOWN RACES

Stephen Foster

1. Camp-town la-dies sing this song,
2. Came down there with my hat caved in,

Doo - dah! Doo - dah!
Doo - dah! Doo - dah!

Camp-town race-track five miles long,
Went back home with a pocket full of tin,

Oh, Doo - dah - day!
Oh, Doo - dah - day!

Chorus

Goin' to run all night,

Goin' to run all day! I'll

bet my money on a bob tail nag,

Some bod - y bet on the bay.

Camptown Races

1. Clap the rhythm pattern as a mystery song.
2. Sing the song and use previous rhythmic experiences (refer to Lesson 11).
3. Create a rhythmic ostinato using various integrated motions to vary the sound while singing the song:

I ⌐‾‾⌐ I I
clap snap snap clap slap knees

Note: This activity will require concentration and coordination. Begin with a simple pattern using repeated motions and progress to more complex motor activities.

Goodbye, Old Paint

1. Teach the song. There are many verses to be found in folk songbooks or music textbooks.

2. The rhythmic activities will vary with this song because the beat is in three. Sing the song, sway back and forth to the pulse (one to the measure).
3. Sing the song, sway the pulse, step the beat.

   • How many steps did the class have to take to each sway? *3*
   • Does the song start on the first beat? *No*
   • What is the name of the beat before 1? *anacrusis*

INTRODUCE THE CHART

1. Clap one of the patterns on the chart. Let the class identify the pattern by number (1, 2, or 3). Ask the student who identified the pattern to sing the tone syllables with hand signals. Can the class identify the song? Sing the song using hand signals for the phrase on the chart.

2. Continue through the chart.

   • Clap the pattern
   • Identify the song
   • Sing the tone syllables with hand signals
   • Sing the song, using hand signals for the phrase on the chart

3. "Goodbye, Old Paint" can be sung in its entirety with hand signals if you introduce the low *sol* (*sol*₁) by rote. Use the vertical scale (see Lesson 17) to show the spatial relationship of the interval.

4. Establish the starting pitch. Keep the beat on the chart, but *do not* sing. Now, ask the class to sing each phrase on the chart with hand signals. Can they sing the chart unassisted? Not everyone in the class will be successful with this activity.

5. Make the hand signals for one of the phrases on the chart but *do not* sing. Ask for volunteers to sing the phrase with syllables or words and hand signals.

ADDITIONAL ACTIVITIES

1. Use a rhythm pattern contained in one of the songs as an instrumental ostinato. Encourage musical discrimination. For example:

   • "Are You Sleeping?"
     triangle:
     small woodblock:

   • "Camptown Races"
     woodblock:
     tambourine:

   • "Goodbye, Old Paint"
     woodblock:
     jingle bells:

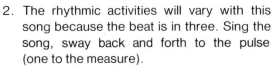

3. GOODBYE, OLD PAINT

Cowboy Song

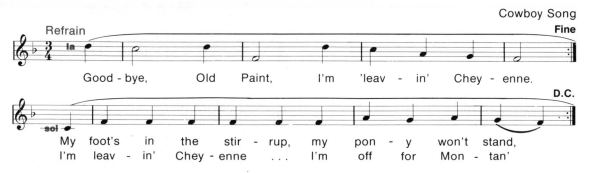

Good - bye, Old Paint, I'm 'leav - in' Chey - enne.

My foot's in the stir - rup, my pon - y won't stand,
I'm leav - in' Chey - enne . . . I'm off for Mon - tan'

2. Sing "Are You Sleeping?"

- Choose one phrase to sing as a melodic ostinato.
- Combine melodic and instrumental ostinatos while one group sings the song.
- Play the melodic ostinato on the bells or recorder.

‖: Are you sleeping :‖   ‖: C D E C :‖

‖: Brother John :‖   ‖: E F G ⁊ :‖

‖: Morning bells are ringing :‖   ‖: G A G F E C :‖

‖: Ding, ding, dong :‖   ‖: C G͵ C ⁊ :‖

This activity can be done with most rounds.

3. As the class becomes more confident in performing ostinatos, let them create their own.

- Establish a rhythm pattern
- Add tone syllables to the rhythm pattern
- Sing the melodic pattern
- Divide the class. One group sings the melody, the other group sings the ostinato.

*Note: This activity will require some experimentation with sound. Which intervals are pleasing to the ear and which intervals create a **dissonance**? Remember, dissonance is not always as unpleasant to students as it is to adults.*

4. Proceed to Chart 41.

Sing A Song

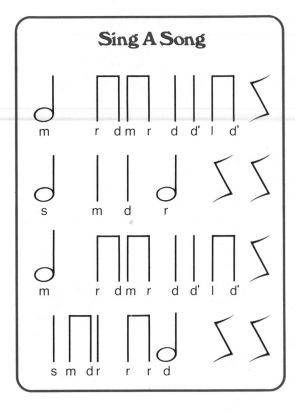

Sing A Song

m r d m r d d' l d'

s m d r

m r d m r d d' l d'

s m d r r r d

OLD FOLKS AT HOME

Stephen Foster

1. Way down up — on the Swan — ee riv—er, Far, far a — way,
2. All up and down the whole cre—a—tion, Sad — ly I roam,

There's where my heart is turn — ing ev—er, There's where the old folks
Still long—ing for the old plan—ta—tion, And for the old folks at home.

All the world is sad and drear — y, Ev — ery — where I roam,

Oh! Friends, see how my heart grows wear—y, Far from the old folks at home.

PREPARATION FOR THE CHART

1. Teach the song. (Only a portion of the song appears on the chart.)

   Note: Let the class decide which word they will use for the last section of the song.

   "Oh, <u>Johnny</u>, how my heart . . ."

   "Oh, <u>children</u>, how my heart . . ."

2. Sing the song and use previous rhythmic experiences (refer to Lesson 11).

3. Prepare the class by echo singing various patterns using the high *do* (*do'*) and *la*.

Teacher sings with hand signals	Class echoes with hand signals

⊓ l　⊓ l　　　　⊓　　⊓ l
d r m　s l d¹　　d r m　s l d¹

l l　⊓ l　　　　l l　⊓ l
d¹ l　s m d　　d¹ l　s m d

⊓ ⊓ ⊓ l　　　⊓ ⊓ ⊓ l
d¹ l d¹ l s m r　d¹ l d¹ l s m r

4. For the more musically mature class, try two-hand singing, using the above intervals (see Lesson 29). Ask the class to name the interval *do¹–la.* Is it major or minor? *minor third—three half steps* See Chart 17 or Chart 24.)

INTRODUCE THE CHART

1. Ask for a volunteer to clap the first line of the chart with rhythm syllables. If the student is correct, the class will echo. Continue through the entire chart with a different student for each line.
2. Step the beat of the entire chart while clapping the rhythm pattern and saying rhythm syllables.

   Note: If the song was taught prior to the introduction to the chart, the rhythm pattern can be used as a mystery song.

3. Sing the first line of the chart with the class using tone syllables and hand signals. Take note of the spatial relationships of the intervals, particularly from low *do* to high *do* (*d–d¹*) and high *do* to *la* (*d¹–l*). Continue through the entire chart.

4. Choose individual students to sing one line of the chart with hand signals.
5. Sing the entire chart with words and hand signals while stepping the beat.

OTHER SONGS TO USE

- "My Lord, What a Morning"

  l ♩　⊓ l｜l ♩ ≹
  m m　r m d d

- "Good Night, Ladies" (refrain)

  l. ♪ l l｜l l l ≹
  m r d r m m m

- "Are You Sleeping?"

  l l l l｜l l l l
  d r m d d r m d

ADDITIONAL ACTIVITIES

1. This song has a very interesting melodic contour. Ask the class to make a picture of the melody in the air, using large arm movements. This picture can be put on paper.

   Phrase 1 ⌇⌒⌇　　Phrase 2: ⌒⌇

2. Discuss the similarities and differences of the melody (form):

   - Phrase 1—A
   - Phrase 2—B
   - Phrase 3—A
   - Phrase 4—C

   Continue through the entire song. Geometric figures could also be used in this activity to portray the similarities and differences.

3. Proceed to Chart 42.

What Do You Hear?

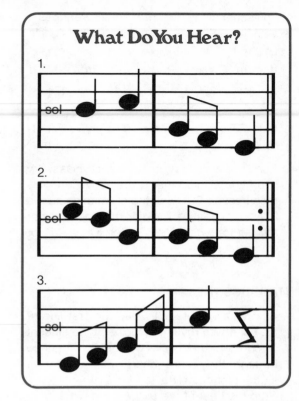

Note: Charts 42, 43, and 44 will act as a culmination to the higher grades charts. Several of the concepts will be presented for review.

PREPARATION FOR THE CHART

1. Ask the class, "What does the double bar tell you?" ‖ *end of the song* What does the double bar with dots mean? ‖: :‖ *repeat*
2. Review the position of the notes on the staff. "If *sol* is on the third line, where is *la*?" *space above* sol *or fourth space* Continue through the rest of the syllables.
3. Review the names of the intervals.

   - *sol–mi* minor third
   - *sol–la* major second
   - *la–mi* perfect fourth
   - *mi–do* major third
   - *re–do* major second
   - *sol–do* perfect fifth
   - *do¹–la* minor third
   - *do–do¹* octave

INTRODUCE THE CHART

1. Choose one student to clap the rhythm pattern of one of the lines on the chart. Ask the class to identify the pattern. Continue through the chart.
2. Ask a volunteer to sing one of the lines on the chart with syllables and hand signals. If the student is confident, let him or her establish the starting pitch. The class will echo with tone syllables and hand signals only if the student is correct and observes all the symbols on the chart. If he or she is incorrect, the class will remain silent, and the student can either correct the mistake or choose another student.
3. Sing one of the lines of the chart on a neutral syllable, for example, "loo," with hand signals. Can they identify the phrase on the chart?
4. Sing various lines on the chart and deliberately alter either the rhythm pattern or one of the intervals. Tell the class they may echo only if the melodic pattern is on the chart.

ADDITIONAL ACTIVITIES

1. Sing or play on the bells, piano, or recorder a melodic pattern using the pentatonic scale (*do–re–mi–sol–la–do¹*). Establish the position of the starting note. The class will write the pattern on the staff, using either staff paper or individual staff charts. Begin with one-measure patterns. Later, use two measures with more difficult rhythms. Sing or play:

2. Choose individuals to sing a melodic pattern with hand signals using the pentatonic scale. The class will echo.
3. Play on the bells, piano, or sing on a neutral syllable ("loo") various intervals. Establish the starting pitch by telling the class the first tone will be *sol*.

Teacher plays or sings	Class sings with hand signals
(G is *sol*)	
G–E G–E	*sol–mi,* minor third
A–E A–E	*la–mi,* perfect fourth
A–G A–G	*la–sol,* major second

Continue through the intervals that have been presented in this book. You may have to reinforce the starting tone syllable. A more difficult activity would be to play or sing the intervals ascending, for example, E to G, C to E, and so on.

EVALUATION OF RHYTHMIC AND PERCEPTUAL SKILLS

Psychomotor Development and Perception

1. Can the students feel the beat of the song with motor activities such as

   - stepping?
   - walking?
   - clapping?
   - swaying?

2. Can they feel the phrase of the song with motor activities?

3. Can they make pictures of the melody, showing the direction, up and down, and the positions of the intervals and phrases?

Aural Acuity and Perception

1. Can the students hear and recognize the interval of the major second when it is played or sung within a familiar song? When it is played on an instrument?
2. Can they hear the interval of the major second with inner hearing while observing only hand signals?

Visual Acuity and Perception

1. Can the students recognize and sing the interval of the major second while reading and singing the charts?
2. Are they aware of the position of the intervals on the staff?

Brooms

Brooms

do   mi

sol   do'

Brooms, brooms,
Brooms, brooms.
What are they for?
What are they for?
Sweeping, sweeping,
Sweeping, sweeping the
Floors, floors.

BROOMS

Traditional Dutch Round

sol
do
Brooms, brooms, brooms, brooms,

3   3
What are they for?   What are they for?

Sweep-ing, sweep-ing, sweep-ing,

3
sweep-ing   the floors,   floors.

PREPARATION FOR THE CHART

1. Teach the song. This is an adaptation of an old Dutch round that can be found in many textbooks under the title "De Besom!"
2. Sing the song and use previous rhythmic activities. The class will enjoy stepping the rhythm pattern. Use flash cards to change the activities:

   • clap—Phrase 1
   • step—Phrase 2
   • feel—Phrase 3
   • sing—Phrase 4

3. Sing the song as a round in two, three, or four parts.
4. Step or walk the song as a two-part round. This can be done by singing and stepping the pattern, or stepping the pattern only.

INTRODUCE THE CHART

1. Read and clap the rhythm pattern with rhythm syllables.
2. Read and clap the rhythm pattern. Step the beat.
3. Clap the beat. Step the rhythm pattern.
4. Speak the words. Clap the beat. Step the rhythm pattern.
5. Read the chart but do not sing. Use hand signals for the tone syllables on each phrase, while keeping the beat.
6. Sing the song with hand signals and tone syllables.
7. Sing the song with hand signals and tone syllables. Dramatize the intervals:

   "Brooms"—fists on the floor
   "What are they for?"—slap the knees, rising slightly

- "Sweeping"—stand up and clap hands
- "Floors"—fists over head

8. Repeat the last activity using words.
9. Divide the class into two, three, or four groups. Sing the song as a round and use body motions (Activity 7).

ADDITIONAL ACTIVITIES

1. *Game:*

   Equipment: A broom that is fairly new and stiff so that it bounces straight up when dropped.

   Formation: Circle, one student holding the broom in his or her right hand. Sing the song beginning slowly.

   - "Brooms, brooms"—bounce broom two times with right hand and pass quickly to left hand.
   - "Brooms"—bounce broom once with left hand.
   - "Brooms"—bounce and pass broom to person on the left without losing the beat.

   Continue singing the song, passing the broom on every fourth beat:

   | | | | |
   R.H. R.H. L.H. (pass)

   ⌒3   ⌒3
   ┌┬┐ | ┌┬┐ |
   R.H. R.H. L.H. (pass)

If one student drops the broom or loses the beat, he or she must take a seat. Increase the tempo, getting faster on each repeat until the game ends with only two children remaining. The class continues singing the song.

2. A variation of this game is to choose four students to sing the song as a four-part round. The first student sings "Brooms, brooms, brooms, brooms," while bouncing the broom and passes the broom on the fourth beat while continuing to sing the song. The second student sings "Brooms, brooms, brooms, brooms," and so on.

EVALUATION OF RHYTHMIC AND PERCEPTUAL SKILLS

Psychomotor Development and Perception

Are the students increasing their ability to coordinate various activities?

Musical Development and Social Maturity

Are the students approaching new musical activities with enthusiasm and enjoyment?

Note: If you feel that the students are not successful while performing an activity, it would be wise to review previous charts. This will insure their success and add to their enjoyment.

Rain, Rain, Go Away

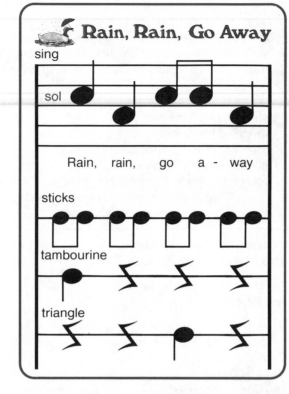

Rain, Rain, Go Away

sing

sol

Rain, rain, go a - way

sticks

tambourine

triangle

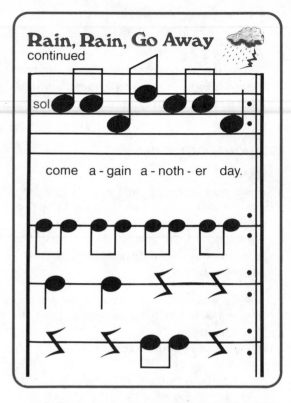

Rain, Rain, Go Away

continued

sol

come a - gain a - noth - er day.

In this lesson we introduce score reading. When the staves are connected by a line on the left-hand side, they are all read and played or sung simultaneously. It is helpful and interesting to show the class an instrumental score, so that they can see how the instrumental parts are written on a conductor's score.

INTRODUCE THE CHARTS

1. Establish the pitch for *sol* and sing the top line of both charts with the class. Use tone syllables and hand signals. Observe the repeat signs.
2. Sing the top line with words and hand signals.
3. Sing the top line of the chart with words and tap the beat on the desk.
4. Ask one student to clap the rhythm pattern of the second line of both charts while the class taps the beat softly.
5. Sing the song and tap the second line on the desk.
6. Choose one student to read and clap the third line of both charts, observing the rests and repeat signs. The class softly taps the beat and sings the song.
7. Repeat Activity 6 for the last line of the chart.
8. Divide the class into four groups.

   - Group 1 sings the song
   - Group 2 taps the second line
   - Group 3 claps the third line
   - Group 4 raps (knuckles) the fourth line.

   Establish the beat by saying, "One, two, ready, sing."
9. Distribute the rhythm instruments to indi-
vidual students (the orchestra). Establish the beat. The class sings the song, while individuals play the pattern on the charts.
10. Create words to the patterns on Lines 3 and 4:

    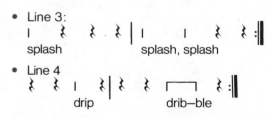

    - Line 3:
      splash   splash, splash
    - Line 4
      drip   drib—ble

Divide the class into three groups. Group 1 sings and taps Lines 1 and 2; Group 2 speaks Line 3; Group 3 speaks Line 4.

Note: Not all classes will be able to perform this highly integrated activity, but they will enjoy trying.

ADDITIONAL ACTIVITIES

Note: This song uses only notes contained within the pentatonic scale. Let the class create a two-measure melodic pattern using the notes of the pentatonic scale (d–r–m–s–l–d¹).

1. Choose one student to clap a two-measure rhythm pattern.

   - Put the pattern on the chalkboard.
   - Create a melody with tone syllables. Put the letters under the rhythm pattern:

   | ♩ 𝄽 ☐ ♩ | ♩ ♩ ♩ 𝄽 :‖
   d   m m s   l s m

   - Create words to the melodic pattern:

   | ♩ 𝄽 ☐ ♩ | ♩ ♩ ♩ 𝄽 :‖
   Rain com—ing down,   cold and gray.

   Divide the class into two groups. Group 1 sings the chart; Group 2 sings the original melody with words. Several original melodies can be used while one group sings the song and the other group reads the chart with tapping and instruments.

2. Instruments, such as bells, piano, recorder, or song flute can be used with Activity 1. Create melodic patterns using the notes of the pentatonic scale.

3. Use poetry suitable to the grade level.

   - Discover and write the rhythm pattern of a poem on the chalkboard.
   - Create a melody, using the notes of the pentatonic scale.
   - Create an accompaniment (instrumental ostinatos or melodic ostinatos with words).

EVALUATION AND SUMMARY

Psychomotor Development and Perception

1. Do the students have a strong feeling for the beat and rhythm pattern?
2. Do they perform with confidence integrated rhythmic activities such as

   - singing while stepping or walking?
   - singing while turning the phrase?
   - clapping the pattern while stepping or walking the beat?
   - singing while tapping an ostinato?

Aural Acuity and Perception

1. Can the students hear the intervals within the pentatonic scale? Can they hear and name the

   - Minor third (*sol–mi*)?
   - Major second (*sol–la*)?
   - Perfect fourth (*la–mi*)?
   - Major third (*mi–do*)?
   - Perfect fifth (*sol–do*)?
   - Octave (*do–do¹*)?

2. Can they hear and identify long and short sounds such as

   - ta (♩)?
   - ti-ti (☐)?
   - ta–a (♩)?
   - quarter rest (𝄽)?
   - whole rest (▬)?

Visual Acuity and Perception

1. Can the students read the tone and rhythm symbols on the chart with ease?
2. Can they discover the starting tone when *sol* or *do* is given on the staff?
3. Can they read simple songs containing *do–re–mi–sol–la–do¹*?

Musical Development and Social Maturity

1. Do the students participate and contribute with enthusiasm, involvement, and the beginnings of musical discrimination?
2. Do they identify similarities and differences in a song?
3. Do they derive personal satisfaction from their musical achievement?
4. Are they beginning to think musically at their own level?
5. Are they becoming aware of **meter** (2, 3, or 4)?
6. Are they able to exercise some musical discrimination in their use of

   - dynamics (loud and soft)?
   - appropriate instruments?
   - appropriate tempo?
   - differences in tone quality?

7. Are they developing and using their musical vocabulary?
8. Do they show an increasing willingness to listen and participate?

Hand Signals

Do

Re

Mi

Fa

Sol

La

Ti

Do¹